the **NEW** edition

New Headway

Upper-Intermediate **Student's Book**

Part A Units 1–6

Liz and John Soars

OXFORD
UNIVERSITY PRESS

CONTENTS

UNIT	LANGUAGE FOCUS	VOCABULARY	READING
1 No place like home p6	**The tense system** Simple, continuous, perfect Active and passive p8 **Spoken English** Informal language *Been here two days.* *It's kind of boring.* p8	Compound words *lifestyle, home town, house-proud* p13	A home from home – two people describe their experiences of living abroad (jigsaw) p10
2 Been there, done that! p16	**Present Perfect** *He's been to Vietnam.* *He's been staying in hostels.* **Simple and continuous** *He works for IBM.* *I'm working with Jim.* p18 **Spoken English** Being imprecise *and stuff like that* *sort of* Fillers *I mean like four in the morning.* p24	Hot verbs – *make, do* *make way, do damage* *I could do with a cup of tea.* *He made up the whole story.* p23	'Paradise Lost' – how tourism is destroying the object of its affection p19
3 What a story! p26	**Narrative tenses** Past Simple, Past Continuous, Past Perfect active and passive p26 **Spoken English** News and responses *Did you read that story about …?* *You're kidding!* *I don't get it.* p28 The use of *like* *It was like really out of the ordinary.* p32	Books and films *It's a thriller set in New York.* *Has it been made into a film?* *It stars Harrison Ford.* p29	Chapter One of *The Blind Assassin*, a novel by Margaret Atwood p30

Stop and check 1   Teacher's Book p164

UNIT	LANGUAGE FOCUS	VOCABULARY	READING
4 Nothing but the truth p34	**Questions and negatives** *Who gave you that?* *Haven't I told you before?* *Who with?* *I don't think you're right.* *I hope not.* p35 **Spoken English** The question *How come?* *How come you don't eat meat?* p36	Prefixes *disbelief, incredible, improbable* Antonyms in context *successful/failure* *generous/meanness* p42	'Diana and Elvis shot JFK!' – three of the world's most popular conspiracy theories (jigsaw) p38
5 An eye to the future p44	**Future forms** *will, going to, shall* *is staying* *leaves* *will be doing* *will have done* p45 **Spoken English** The word *thing* *How are things?* *The thing is, …* p49	Hot verbs – *take, put* *take years to do sth* *put pressure on sb* *Take your time.* *The shop takes on extra staff.* *Put your cigarette out.* p51	'Nobody listens to us' – a group of young adults are canvassed for their opinions on social issues and their ambitions p48
6 Making it big p54	**Expressions of quantity** *a few, a little, plenty of, hardly any* p55 **Spoken English** Informal expressions of quantity *loads of, masses of* p56	Words with variable stress *'export* and *ex'port* *re'fuse* and *'refuse* p60	A profile of two famous brands – Starbucks and Apple Macintosh (jigsaw) p58

Stop and check 2   Teacher's Book p167

Tapescripts p70   **Grammar Reference** p79   **Phonetic symbols** p95

LISTENING	SPEAKING	EVERYDAY ENGLISH	WRITING
'Things I miss from home' – people describe what they miss when they travel abroad p14	Exchanging information about people who live abroad p10 Discussion – the pros and cons of living abroad p11	Social expressions *Great to see you!* *Don't I know you from somewhere?* p15	Applying for a job A CV and a covering letter p62
An interview with Tashi Wheeler about her travels as a child with her parents, who founded the *Lonely Planet* guides p24	Information gap and roleplay – Tony and Maureen Wheeler p18 Dreams come true – things to do before you die p22	Exclamations *Wow! That's unbelievable!* *How amazing!* *What a brilliant idea!* *What rubbish!* p25	Informal letters Correcting mistakes p64
The money jigsaw – a news item from the BBC's Radio 4 *Today* programme p32	Retelling a news story Responding to a news story p28 Talking about your favourite book or film p29	Showing interest and surprise Echo questions *A new boyfriend?* Reply questions *'He lives in a castle.' 'Does he?'* p33	Narrative writing 1 Using adverbs in narratives *I used to go skiing frequently in winter.* p65
'My most memorable lie!' – people confess to untruths p37	Discussion – good and bad lies p37 Exchanging information about conspiracy theories p38	Being polite *I'm sorry to bother you.* *Could you possibly change a ten-pound note?* p43	Linking ideas Conjunctions *whenever, so that, even though* p66
Arranging to meet – three friends decide a time and a place to get together (jigsaw) p52	Future possibilities in your life p47 Exchanging information about people arranging to meet p52	Telephone conversations Beginning a call Ending a call Roleplay p53	Writing emails Emailing friends *Sorry, can't make next Sat.* p67
Radio advertisements – what's the product? What's the selling point? p57	A lifestyle survey p56 Writing an advert p57 Exchanging information about famous brands p58 A business maze – opening a restaurant p60	Business expressions *Bear with me.* *I'll email the information as an attachment.* Numbers, fractions, decimals, dates, time, phone numbers, sports scores p61	A consumer survey Report writing *FAO: The Managing Director* p68

1

No place like home

The tense system • Informal language • Compound words • Social expressions

TEST YOUR GRAMMAR

1 Which time expressions from the box can be used with the sentences below?

1 My parents met in Paris.
2 They travel abroad.
3 They were working in Canada.
4 I was born in Montreal.
5 My grandparents have lived in Ireland.
6 I wrote to my grandmother.
7 I'm going to work in the US.
8 My brother's flying to Argentina on business.
9 He's been learning Spanish.
10 I'll see you.

when I was born   never   in the 1970s tonight   frequently   for ages   ages ago the other day   in a fortnight's time recently   during a snowstorm   for a year since I was a child   later   sometimes

2 Talk to a partner about yourself and your family using some of the time expressions.

WRITING HOME
Tense revision and informal language

1 Read the letter. Who is writing? Who to? Where is he? What is he complaining about? How old do you think the writer is?

2 Complete the questions. Then ask and answer them with a partner.

1 'How long _____ Max _____ at summer camp?'
  'Just _____.'
2 '_____ he _____ a good time?'
  'No, not really. He _____ very homesick.'
3 'Is this his first time at summer camp?'
  'No, it _____ . He _____ once before. Last year he _____ to Pine Trees.'
4 '_____ he like it at Pine Trees?'
  'Oh, yes, he _____ , very much.'
5 'Why was that?'
  'Because _____.'
6 'What _____ tomorrow?'
  'He _____ pancakes.'
7 'Why _____ his cell phone?'
  'Because _____.'

3 **T 1.1** Listen and check your answers.

Tuesday, 9.00pm

Hi Mom, Hi Dad!
    Been here two days but seems like FOREVER — it's kind of boring and I'm feeling very homesick — more homesick than last year 'cause at Pine Trees we had more exciting stuff to do. Here we have an activity called 'extreme sun tanning', where you sit outside for two hours and do nothing. We also have an activity called 'sitting around playing cards'. Last year we did stuff like archery and mountain biking. I'm still hanging in there, though. Got to go to sleep now. We're making chocolate chip pancakes for breakfast tomorrow.

Love you lots,   **Max** xxxxx

    P.S. Could you send me more money? Oh, and my cell phone. ALL the other kids have their cell phones!

GROVE HILL SUMMER CAMP
MONMOUTH COUNTY

4 Read Sophie's email. What is it about? What do you learn about Sophie's likes and dislikes? Who is Rob? Who do you think Catherine is? Ask and answer the questions with a partner.

1 How long/Sophie/New Zealand?
2 How long/she/Australia?
3 Who/travel/with?
4 Why/like New Zealand?
5 Why/like Kangaroo Island?
6 What/their car like?
7 Which wildlife/already?
8 Where/next?
9 Why/photos?

5 [T 1.2] Listen and check your answers.

LANGUAGE FOCUS

1 Which tenses can you identify in the questions and answers in exercises 2 and 4? Why are they used?

2 **Informal writing** often has lots of colloquial language and words missed out.

kind of boring = quite boring
Been here two days but seems = I've been here two days but
   like FOREVER   it seems like forever.
'cause (US), 'cos (UK) = because

3 Work with a partner. Read the letter and email again.

1 What do 'stuff' and 'hanging in there' mean in Max's letter? Find colloquial words in Sophie's email and express them less colloquially.

2 Find examples where words are missing. Which words?

▶▶ **Grammar Reference pp79–80**

From:	**Sophie Beasely** <sophie.beas@yoohoo.com>
Date:	Wed 16 March, 10.36 am
To:	Robert Elliman
Subject:	New Zealand and missing you.

Hello again Rob!

Nearly two-thirds of the way through the trip now. Still having a great time but missing you like crazy! Been in New Zealand nearly a week and have met up with Catherine at last. Like it lots here. It has many advantages over Australia, the main ones being that it's smaller and cooler. Still, 3 weeks in Oz had its good points, despite the 44 degree heat! Kangaroo Island (near Adelaide) was my favourite place – loads of wildlife – did I tell you I'd seen some platypus there?

Here in New Zealand, first thing we did was buy a car. Went to the classy sounding 'Del's Cars' and, using our extensive mechanical knowledge (ha! ha!), chose a car and gave it a thorough examination (i.e. checked the lights worked & the glove box could hold 8 large bars of chocolate). It's going OK so far, but sometimes makes strange noises! We're taking things nice and slowly now. Have already seen dolphins, whales, and enormous albatrosses.

So – that's it for now. We're heading up the west coast next. Thanks for all your emails – it's great to get news from home. Can't wait to see you. I'm sending you some photos so you won't forget what I look like!

Love you. Wish, wish, wish you were here!

Sophie xxxxx (Catherine sends love too)

PRACTICE

Identifying the tenses

1 Complete the tense charts. Use the verb *work* for the active and *make* for the passive.

ACTIVE	Simple	Continuous
Present	he **works**	we **are working**
Past	she	I
Future	they	you
Present Perfect	we	she
Past Perfect	I **had worked**	you
Future Perfect	they	he **will have been working**

PASSIVE	Simple	Continuous
Present	it **is made**	they **are being made**
Past	it	it
Future	they	
Present Perfect	they	
Past Perfect	it	
Future Perfect	they **will have been made**	

2 **T 1.3** Listen to the lines of conversation and discuss what the context might be. Listen again and identify the tenses. Which lines have contractions?

He's been working such long hours recently. He never sees the children.

– *Could be a wife talking about her husband.*

– *Present Perfect Continuous, Present Simple.*

– *He's (He has) been working …*

Discussing grammar

3 Compare the meaning in the pairs of sentences. Which tenses are used? Why?

1 Klaus **comes** from Berlin.
   Klaus **is coming** from Berlin.
2 You**'re** very kind. Thank you.
   You**'re being** very kind. What do you want?
3 What **were** you **doing** when the accident happened?
   What **did** you **do** when the accident happened?
4 I**'ve lived** in Singapore for five years.
   I **lived** in Singapore for five years.
5 When we arrived, he **tidied** the flat.
   When we arrived, he**'d tidied** the flat.
6 We**'ll have** dinner at 8.00, shall we?
   Don't call at 8.00. We**'ll be having** dinner.
7 How much **are** you **paying** to have the house painted?
   How much **are** you **being paid** to paint the house?
8 How **do you do**?
   How **are you doing**?

Talking about you

4 Complete these sentences with your ideas.

1 At weekends I often …
2 My parents have never …
3 I don't think I'll ever …
4 I was saying to a friend just the other day that …
5 I hate Mondays because …
6 I'd just arrived home last night when …
7 I was just getting ready to go out this morning when …
8 I've been told that our teacher …
9 In my very first English lesson I was taught …
10 The reason I'm learning English is because …

T 1.4 Listen and compare. What are the responses?

5 Work with a partner. Listen to each other's sentences and respond.

SPOKEN ENGLISH Missing words out

Which words are missing in these lines from conversations?

1 Heard about Jane and John splitting up?
2 Leaving already? What's wrong?
3 Failed again? How many times is that?
4 Sorry I'm late. Been waiting long?
5 Doing anything interesting this weekend?
6 Like the car! When did you get it?
7 Bye Jo! See you later.
8 Just coming! Hang on!
9 Want a lift? Hop in.
10 Seen Jim lately?

Read the lines aloud to your partner and make suitable responses.

T 1.5 Listen and compare.

A long-distance phone call

6 Read through these lines of a phone conversation. Kirsty is calling her father. Where do you think she is? Why is she there? Where is he? Work with a partner to complete her father's lines in the conversation.

D ...
K Dad! It's me, Kirsty.
D ...
K I'm fine, but still a bit jet-lagged.
D ...
K It's nine hours ahead. I just can't get used to it. Last night I lay awake all night, and then today I nearly fell asleep at work in the middle of a meeting.
D ...
K It's early days but I think it's going to be really good. It's a big company but everybody's being so kind and helpful. I've been trying to find out how everything works.
D ...
K I've seen a bit. It just seems such a big, busy city. I don't see how I'll ever find my way round it.
D ...
K No, it's nothing like London. It's like nowhere else I've ever been – masses of huge buildings, underground shopping centres, lots of taxis and people – so many people – but it's so clean. No litter on the streets or anything.
D ...
K Well, for the time being I've been given a tiny apartment, but it's in a great part of town.
D ...
K That's right. I won't be living here for long. I'll be offered a bigger place as soon as one becomes available, which is good 'cos this one really is tiny, but at least it's near to where I'm working.
D ...
K Walk! You're kidding! It's not *that* close. It's a short subway ride away. And the trains come so regularly – it's a really easy journey, which is good 'cos I start work very early in the morning.
D ...
K Again it's too early to say. I think I really will be enjoying it all soon. I'm sure it's going to be a great experience. It's just that I miss everyone at home so much.
D ...
K I will. I promise. And you email me back with all your news. I just love getting news from home. Give everyone my love. Bye.
D ...

T 1.6 Listen and compare. Identify some of the tenses used in the conversation.

▶▶▶ **WRITING** Applying for a job *p62*

READING AND SPEAKING
A home from home

1 Why do people go to live abroad? Make a list of reasons and discuss with your class.

2 You are going to read about Ian Walker-Smith, who moved to Chile, and Thomas Creed, who moved to Korea.

Which of these lines from the articles do you think are about Chile (**C**) and which about Korea (**K**)?

1 ☐ As we're 2,600 m above sea level, I easily get puffed when I'm exercising.

2 ☐ Soccer is a really big deal here ever since they hosted the 2002 World Cup.

3 ☐ … we converse in what we call 'Espanglish' …

4 ☐ … learning Chinese characters stinks.

5 ☐ … its surrounding mines are said to make more money than any other city.

6 ☐ I can eat spicy food like *kimchee* …

7 ☐ It's also normal to roll out mattresses and sleep on the floor.

8 ☐ We now have a pleasant walkway along the seafront.

3 Divide into two groups.

Group A Read about Ian on this page.
Group B Read about Thomas on p12.

Check your answers to exercise 2.

4 Answer the questions about Ian or Thomas.

1 Where did he go to live abroad? Why?
2 How long has he been there?
3 What does he do there?
4 What do you learn about his family?
5 What is the new home town like?
6 Have there been any difficulties?
7 In what ways is he 'in the middle of nowhere'?
8 Does he feel at home in his new home?
9 What does he like and dislike about his new life?
10 What does he miss?

5 Find a partner from the other group. Compare your answers. Who do you think is happier about the move? Which new home would you prefer?

Expat tales

IAN WALKER-SMITH IN CHILE

Ian Walker-Smith comes from Crewe, England, but now lives and works in Chile. He's married to a Chilean woman,
05 Andrea, and works for a European astronomical agency in the town of Paranal.

Ian says: ❝ I work shifts of eight days in Paranal, and get six to rest at home – in my case, the mining town of Antofagasta, a harrowing
10 two-hour drive away on the coast. It takes a real toll, being so far from Andrea. I miss her when I'm away.

Where he works

I work at Paranal Observatory, where every night the boundaries of our universe are probed by four of the world's largest telescopes. I'm part of a 12-strong I.T. team which looks after everything from
15 satellite ground stations to desktop support. My role is to make sure the computers run 24/7. As Paranal is in the middle of nowhere – up a mountain in the desert – the sky is truly amazing. As we're 2,600 m above sea level, I easily get puffed when I'm exercising and each time I arrive for a week on shift, I can't think straight or fast for the first
20 day or so.

Why he moved

I decided to move to Chile four years ago when I was a 25-year-old with itchy feet (and wanted to get out of the way of an ex-girlfriend!). I was working for Littlewoods Home Shopping Group, and one day a colleague pointed out this job in Chile. We both thought it would be
25 a good idea, but I was the one who put a CV together.

Life in Chile

Landing at Santiago airport was my first experience of language being such a barrier. I couldn't speak more than a handful of words in Spanish, and would you believe that my baggage had got lost! So my first couple of hours in Chile were spent trying to locate my missing
30 possessions. Today I can order food in restaurants and argue with mechanics about my car, but I can't really make myself understood on any deeper level. I can't get my thoughts across as a native speaker could. Andrea speaks pretty good English, and we converse in what we call 'Espanglish' – at least we can understand each other.

35 Antofagasta, the town where we have made our home, was once described in a Chilean advertising campaign as the 'Pearl of the North'. Let's just say that it's hardly a tourist destination (which is pretty much what you'd say about my home town, Crewe!). Antofagasta and its surrounding mines are said to make more money
40 for Chile than any other city. During my time here, some money has been put back into the city. The municipal beach has been much improved. We now have a pleasant walkway along the seafront.

What he misses

Even after four years, I don't feel I belong. Over Christmas I went back to the UK for a month's holiday – on landing at Heathrow, I felt at home
45 straight away. What I miss most is greenery. My own culture still fits me like the winter gloves I left behind when I came to work in the desert sun. Shame I can't say the same of my old winter trousers ...

Language work

Study the texts again and answer the questions about these expressions. Explain the meanings to a partner who read the other text.

Ian in Chile
1 *It takes a real toll,* ... l.10
   What takes a toll? On what or who?
2 **... the computers run 24/7.* l.16
   How long do the computers operate?
3 **I easily get puffed* ... l.18
   When and why does he get puffed?
4 **... itchy feet* ... l.24
   Why did he get itchy feet?
5 *... winter gloves* ... l.48
   What still fits him like winter gloves?

Thomas in Korea
1 **... I'm really into soccer.* l.07
   Is he a soccer fan?
2 **... a really big deal* ... l.08
   What is a really big deal? Why?
3 **... doesn't get it.* l.09
   Who doesn't get what? Why not?
4 **... a big shot.* l.17
   Who is a big shot? What makes him a big shot?
5 **... the bad guy is beating him up.* l.53
   Who is the bad guy beating up?

Express all the lines marked with an asterisk (*) in more formal English.

What do you think?

Work in groups.

- Close your eyes and think about your country. What would you miss most if you went to live abroad? Compare ideas.
- Make a list of the disadvantages of moving abroad. Then for every disadvantage (−) try to find an advantage (+).

  ⊖ The language barrier – maybe you don't speak the language.

  ⊕ But this is an opportunity to learn a new language.

- Have any of your friends or family gone to live in a foreign country? Why?
- Do you know anyone who has come to live in your country from another country? Why? Do they have any problems?
- Which other countries would you like to live in for a while? Why?

Expat tales

'I'm part of the group now. The only difference is I have brown hair and blue eyes,' says Thomas Creed, an eleven-year-old originally from Boston, Massachusetts.

Thomas says: ❝ These days I'm really into soccer. Soccer is a really big deal here ever since they hosted the 2002 World Cup. But Dad doesn't get it. I wasn't a soccer fan
10 either when I first came to Seoul six years ago. Like my dad, I was a big basketball fan – still am – watching all the games Dad taped, cheering for the Celtics. But now, me and my friends play soccer all the time. It's hard not to get addicted! My best friend Dong-won and I cut out photos
15 of David Beckham and trade them like baseball cards.

Why he moved

My dad's an officer in the US Army, but he wasn't always such a big shot. He had 'tours of duty', which means he's had to move around whether he liked it or not. He's lived in places like Germany, Vietnam, and Saudi Arabia.
20 My mom and I always stayed back in Boston. She's a scientist. But then my dad and my big brother Patrick both got transferred to Korea – Patrick's ten years older than me, and he's in the Army, too. So our whole family moved over. Seoul's cool. There are millions of places
25 called 'PC rooms' where you can play tons of Internet games. The city's a lot bigger than Boston, too, and way more crowded and busy. I didn't like that at first. I couldn't understand what anyone was saying, and people here don't always
30 smile at strangers like they do back in the US. I felt lonely, like I was in the middle of nowhere.

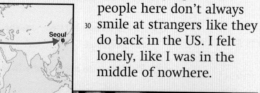

Life in Korea

Life's different here. Most homes don't have radiators –
35 the heat comes up through the floor instead. It's done like this because most Koreans eat cross-legged on floor mats. It's easier than using chairs but it gives my father leg cramps. It's also normal to roll out mattresses and sleep on the floor. That's how I sleep over at Dong-
40 won's house. Dong-won's great and helped me a lot when I first started elementary school here. I was five and didn't know anything or anybody and was pretty scared. I even made my dad wait for me in the next room. Now I can speak Korean fluently, but learning
45 Chinese characters stinks. I always do badly on those tests. I can eat spicy foods like kimchee, and I've read a lot of Korean books and stories, which I like.

What he misses

What I miss most are American comics. I know it's
50 stupid 'cause there are lots of comics here, but they're different. They don't have superheroes like Spiderman, who always has something cool to say, even when the bad guy is beating him up. Also, I wish basketball was more popular. I love soccer but no one understands
55 how *awesome a *'slam dunk' can be.

But I like living here. The people are really nice, and maybe I'll be a translator one day … or even better, a great soccer player like David Beckham. ❞

* incredible
* when a basketball player jumps up above the basket and pushes the ball down into it

VOCABULARY AND PRONUNCIATION
House and home

> **Compound nouns and adjectives**
>
> Words can combine to make new words.
>
> 1 Look at the examples. Which are nouns and which are adjectives?
>
> **life**   *lifestyle   lifelong   life-size*
> *life expectancy   life insurance*
>
> Your dictionary can tell you when to use hyphens and spaces.
>
> 2 Read the compounds aloud. Which words are stressed?
>
> 3 Look at the texts on pp10–12 and find some compound nouns and adjectives.

'*Please turn it down – Daddy's trying to do your homework.*'

1 How many new words can you make by combining a word on the left with a word on the right? Which are nouns and which are adjectives?

home
house

work	made	wife	sick	proud
page	plant	town	coming	
less	grown	bound	warming	

2 **T 1.7** Listen to the conversations. After each one, discuss these questions. Who is talking to who? What about? Which compounds from exercise 1 are used?

3 Complete these lines from the conversations.

1 I'm going away for two weeks. Do you think you could possibly water my _____ for me?

2 Don't worry, I know how _____ you are. I'll make sure everything stays clean and tidy.

3 Let's give her a spectacular _____ party when she gets back from New York.

4 Me? I'm just a _____. Four kids, _____ cakes, and _____ vegetables!

5 We're having a _____ party on the 12th. Can you come? I'll give you our new address.

6 Mind you, with it being much bigger, there's much more _____ to do!

7 Her grandmother's sick and _____, so they have to go and help.

4 **T 1.8** Practise saying the lines in exercise 3 with correct stress and intonation. Listen and check. Try to remember more of each conversation and act some of them out with a partner.

5 Work in groups. Make compounds by combining words from one of the boxes in **A** with as many words as possible from **B**. Use your dictionary to help.

A		B
book	tea	pill line mail way case bell
computer	sleeping	light air house bag software
air	door	escape office food poisoning
junk	open	pot step rest alarm shelf
food	fire	program processor
word	head	

Share your words with a different group and explain the meanings.

 SONG *Don't leave home* Teacher's Book *p143*

LISTENING AND SPEAKING
Things I miss from home

1 When have you spent time away from home? Where did you go? Why? Did you have a good time? What did you miss from home?

2 Write down one thing that you missed on a piece of paper, and give it to your teacher. You will use these later.

3 **T 1.9** Listen to some people talking about the things they miss most when they are away from home. Take notes and compare them in groups.

	What they miss	Other information
Andrew		
Helen		
Gabriele		
Paul		
Sylvia		
Chris		

4 **T 1.9** Read the lines below. Then listen again. Who is speaking? What do the words in *italics* refer to?

1 That sounds very silly but I like to see *them* from time to time.

2 I can't bear to wake up in the morning and be without *them* …

3 … *it*'s all very reassuring, even if *he*'s telling something dreadful.

4 And I am there, waving *the aerial* around and twiddling *the knob* …

5 *They* can be quite wonderful because you don't need to worry about traffic …

6 … and spend … a large part of *the day* just sitting around reading the paper …

5 Read aloud the things that were written down in exercise 2. Guess who wrote them. Whose is the funniest? The most interesting?

EVERYDAY ENGLISH
Social expressions and the music of English

1 Work with a partner. Match a line in **A** with a line in **B**.

A	B
1 Great to see you. Come on in.	a Let me see. No, actually, I don't think I'll bother with dessert.
2 Excuse me, don't I know you from somewhere?	b I was just passing and thought I'd drop in.
3 What d'you mean you're not coming?	c Really! That's a drag. I was hoping to meet her.
4 I think I'll have the chocolate mousse. What about you?	d No, I don't think so.
5 My flatmate can't make it to your party.	e Well, I just don't feel up to going out tonight.
6 How come you're not having a holiday this year?	f Fantastic! I knew you'd swing it for us.
7 You'll make yourself ill if you carry on working at that pace.	g We just can't afford it.
8 I've got you the last two tickets for the show.	h That's as maybe but I have to get this finished by Friday.

T 1.10 Listen and check. Pay particular attention to the stress and intonation. Practise the lines with your partner.

> ### Music *of* English ♪♩
>
> **T 1.11** The 'music' of a language is made up of three things.
>
> 1 Intonation – the up and down of the voice:
>
> *Excuse me!*   *Really?*
>
> 2 Stress – the accented syllables in individual words:
>
> *chocolate   fantastic   dessert*
>
> 3 Rhythm – the stressed syllables over a group of words:
>
> *What d'you mean you're not coming?*

2 **T 1.12** Listen to the conversation and concentrate on the 'music'. Who are the people? Do they know each other? Where are they?

3 Work with a partner. Look at the conversation on p89. Take the roles of **A** and **B** and read the conversation aloud, using the stress shading to help you.

T 1.12 Listen again and repeat the lines one by one. Practise the conversation again with your partner.

4 The stressed words are given in these conversations. Try to complete the lines. Practise saying them as you go.

1

A Excuse ... , ... know you ... somewhere?
B Actually, ... think so.
A ... Gavin's party last week?
B Not me. ... don't know anyone ... Gavin.
A Well, someone ... looked just like ... there.
B Well, that's ... maybe ... certainly wasn't me.
A ... am sorry!

2

A Tony! Hi! Great ... see ... !
B Well, ... just passing ... drop in ... 'hello'.
A ... in! Have ... drink!
B ... sure? ... too busy?
A Never ... busy ... talk ... you.
B Thanks, Jo. ... really nice ... chat.
A Fantastic! Let ... coat.

5 **T 1.13** Listen and compare your ideas and pronunciation.

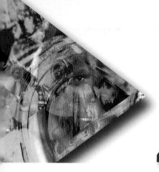

2 Been there, done that!

Present Perfect · Simple and continuous · Hot verbs – *make, do* · Exclamations

TEST YOUR GRAMMAR

1 What is strange about these sentences? What should they be?

1 Columbus has discovered America.
2 Man first walked on the moon.
3 I travelled all my life. I went everywhere.
4 I've learnt English.
5 I've been losing my passport.

2 Which of these verb forms can change from simple to continuous or vice versa? What is the change in meaning?

1 What do you do in New York?
2 I know you don't like my boyfriend.
3 I had a cup of tea at 8.00.
4 Someone's eaten my sandwich.
5 I'm hot because I've been running.

EXPLORERS AND TRAVELLERS
Present Perfect

1 Look at the pictures. Why did people go exploring hundreds of years ago? Why do young people go travelling these days?

2 Read the first and last paragraphs of two articles about Marco Polo and Tommy Willis. Then match the sentences with the correct person. Put **MP** or **TW** in the boxes.

1 ☐ He was born in Venice, the son of a merchant. When he was 17, he set off for China. The journey took four years.

2 ☐ He's visited royal palaces and national parks in South Korea, and climbed to the summit of Mount Fuji in Japan.

3 ☐ He's been staying in cheap hostels, along with a lot of other young people.

4 ☐ His route led him through Persia and Afghanistan.

5 ☐ He was met by the emperor Kublai Khan. He was one of the first Europeans to visit the territory, and he travelled extensively.

6 ☐ 'I've had diarrhoea a few times.' Apart from that, his only worry is the insects. He's been stung all over his body.

7 ☐ He stayed in China for seventeen years. When he left, he took back a fortune in gold and jewellery.

8 ☐ He's been travelling mainly by public transport.

T 2.1 Listen and check. What other information do you learn about the two travellers?

comptevons autres épices.

MARCO POLO 1254–1324

MARCO POLO was the first person to travel the entire 8,000 kilometre length of the Silk Route, the main trade link between Cathay (China) and the West for over two thousand years.

He wrote a book called *The Travels of Marco Polo*, which gave Europeans their first information about China and the Far East.

3 Match a line in **A** with a line in **B**. Practise saying them. Pay attention to contracted forms and weak forms.

A	B
He's been stung	in cheap hostels.
He's visited	all over his body.
He's been staying	a lot of really great people.
I've been	to Vietnam and Japan.
I've met	pickpocketed and mugged.
He's been	royal palaces.

T 2.2 Listen and check.

TOMMY WILLIS backpacker in Asia

Tommy Willis is in Fiji. He's on a nine-month backpacking trip round south-east Asia. He flew into Bangkok five months ago. Since then, he's been to Vietnam, Hong Kong, South Korea, and Japan.

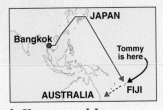

He's looking forward to taking things easy for another week, then setting off again for Australia. 'Once you've got the travel bug, it becomes very hard to stay in the same place for too long,' he said.

LANGUAGE FOCUS

1 What is the main tense used in the sentences about Marco Polo? Why?

What are the main tenses used in the sentences about Tommy Willis? Why?

2 Compare the use of tenses in these sentences.

1 I've read that book. It's good.
I've been reading a great book. I'll lend it to you when I've finished.
I've been reading a lot about Orwell recently. I've just finished his biography.

2 She's been writing since she was 16.
She's written three novels.

3 He's played tennis since he was a kid.
He's been playing tennis since he was a kid.

▶▶ **Grammar Reference p81**

PRACTICE
Questions and answers

1 Read the pairs of questions. First decide who each question is about, Marco Polo or Tommy Willis. Then ask and answer the questions.

1 Where did he go?
Where has he been?

2 How long has he been travelling?
How long did he travel?

3 How did he travel?
How has he been travelling?

4 Who has he met?
Who did he meet?

5 Did he have any problems?
Has he had any problems?

2 Here are the answers to some questions. Write the questions.

About Marco Polo
1 In 1254 in Venice.
2 Four years.
3 For seventeen years.
4 Gold and jewellery.
5 *The Travels of Marco Polo.*

About Tommy Willis
6 For five months. **How long ... away from home?**
7 Thailand, Vietnam, Hong Kong, South Korea, and Japan. **Which ...?**
8 In cheap hostels.
9 A few times. **How many ...?**
10 Yes, once. **Has ...?**

T 2.3 Listen and check your answers.

Discussing grammar

3 Put the verb in the correct tense.
   1 Charles Dickens _____ (write) *Oliver Twist* in 1837.
     I _____ (write) two best-selling crime stories.
     She _____ (write) her autobiography for the past eighteen months.
   2 _____ you ever _____ (try) Mexican food?
     _____ you _____ (try) *chiles rellenos* when you were in Mexico?
   3 How many times _____ you _____ (marry)?
     How many times _____ Henry VIII _____ (marry)?
   4 I _____ (live) in the same house since I was born.
     He _____ (live) with his brother for the past week.
   5 Cinda's very pleased with herself. She _____ finally _____ (give up) smoking. She _____ (try) to give up for years.

Simple and continuous

> ### LANGUAGE FOCUS
>
> **1** Simple verb forms see actions as a complete whole.
> He **works** for IBM.   It **rained** all day yesterday.   I**'ve lost** my passport.
>
> **2** Continuous verb forms see actions in progress, with a beginning and an end.
> I**'m working** with Jim for a couple of days.
> It **was raining** when I woke up.
> The company **has been losing** money for years.
>
> **3** State verbs don't tend to be used in the continuous.
> I **know** Peter well.   I've always **liked** him.
> I **don't understand** what you're saying.
>
> Do you know more verbs like these?
>
> ▶▶ **Grammar Reference pp79–80**

4 Match a line in **A** with a line in **B**. Write 1 or 2 in the box.

A	B
a ☐ Peter comes b ☐ Peter is coming	1 from Switzerland. 2 round at 8.00 tonight.
c ☐ I wrote a report this morning. d ☐ I was writing a report this morning.	1 I'll finish it this afternoon. 2 I sent it off this afternoon.
e ☐ I heard her scream f ☐ I heard the baby screaming	1 when she saw a mouse. 2 all night long.
g ☐ What have you done h ☐ What have you been doing	1 since I last saw you? 2 with my dictionary? I can't find it.
i ☐ I've had j ☐ I've been having	1 a headache all day. 2 second thoughts about the new job.
k ☐ I've known l ☐ I've been getting to know	1 my new neighbours. 2 Anna for over ten years.
m ☐ I've cut n ☐ I've been cutting	1 my finger. It hurts. 2 wood all morning.

▶▶ **WRITING** Informal letters – Correcting mistakes *p64*

Exchanging information

5 Tony and Maureen Wheeler are the founders of the *Lonely Planet* travel guides. There are now over 650 books in the series.

Work with a partner. You each have different information. Ask and answer questions.

Student A Look at p89.
Student B Look at p90.

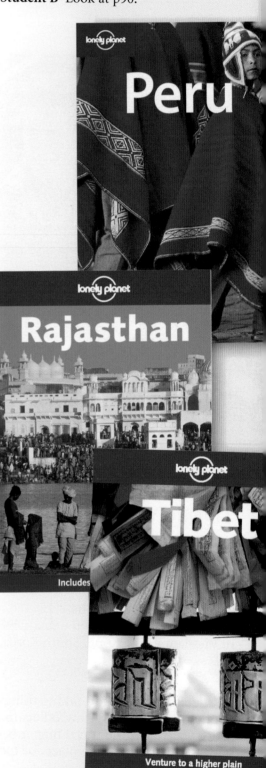

READING AND SPEAKING
Paradise Lost

1 Look at the pictures of tourist destinations in the world. Where are they? Have you been to any of them?

6 Work in groups to prepare an interview with Tony Wheeler. One half of the class will be the interviewers (look at the ideas below), and the other half Tony Wheeler (look at the ideas on p90).

Interviewers

BACKGROUND
Where ... grow up?
What ... father do?

EDUCATION
Where ... school?
Which university ...?

WORK
What work ... after university?

FAMILY
How many children ...?

HOLIDAYS
What ... like doing ...?

LONELY PLANET GUIDES
When ... the first guide book come out?
Where ... idea come from?
What ... the best and worst moment?
What ... secret of your success?
How ... get into travel writing?

FUTURE
Where would you like ...?

2 What are the most important tourist spots in your country? Does tourism cause any problems there?

3 What are the main problems associated with the tourist industry in the world?

Turn to p21.

Paradise lost

What can be done to stop tourism destroying the object of its affection? Maurice Chandler **reports on the boom in world travel.**

On the sun-soaked Mediterranean island of Majorca, the locals are angry. Too late. In the last quarter of the twentieth century, they cashed in on foreign nationals, mainly Germans, wanting to buy up property on their idyllic island. Suddenly it occurred to Majorcans that the island no longer belonged to them. They don't deny tourism's vital contribution to the local economy. The industry has transformed Majorca from one of Spain's poorest parts to the richest in per capita income. But the island's 630,000 inhabitants are increasingly convinced that the 14 million foreign visitors a year are far too much of a good thing. Water is rationed, pollution is worsening, and there is no affordable housing left for them to buy.

On the other side of the world, 250 Filipinos were recently evicted from their homes. Their lake-shore village of Ambulong was cleared by hundreds of police, who demolished 24 houses. The intention of the authorities was to make way for a major business venture – not oil, logging, or mining, but an environmentally-friendly holiday resort.

A growth industry

Tourism is the world's largest and fastest growing industry. In 1950, 25m people travelled abroad; last year it was 750m. The World Tourism Organization estimates that by 2020 1.6bn people will travel each year, spending over two trillion US dollars.

The effects of tourism

To millions of tourists, foreign destinations are exotic paradises, unspoilt, idyllic, and full of local charm. But many of the world's resorts are struggling to cope with relentless waves of tourists, whose demands for ever more swimming pools and golf courses are sucking them dry.

'The issue is massive and global,' says Tricia Barnett, director of Tourism Concern, a charity which campaigns for more responsible approaches to travel. 'Tourists in Africa will be having a shower and then will see a local woman with a pot of water on her head, and they are not making the connection. Sometimes you'll see a village with a single tap, when each hotel has taps and showers in every room.'

The problem is that tourists demand so much water. It has been calculated that a tourist in Spain uses up 880 litres of water a day, compared with 250 litres by a local. An 18-hole golf course in a dry country can consume as much water as a town of 10,000 people. In the Caribbean, hundreds of thousands of people go without piped water during the high tourist season, as springs are piped to hotels.

In 1950, 25m people travelled abroad; last year it was 750m.

Winners and losers

The host country may not see many benefits. In Thailand, 60% of the $4bn annual tourism revenue leaves the country. Low-end package tourists tend to stay at big foreign-owned hotels, cooped up in the hotel compound, buying few local products, and having no contact with the local community other than with the waiters and chambermaids employed by the hotel. 'Mass tourism usually leaves little money inside the country,' says Tricia Barnett. 'Most of the money ends up with the airlines, the tour operators, and the foreign hotel owners.'

These days the industry's most urgent question may be how to keep the crowds at bay. A prime example of this is Italy, where great cultural centres like Florence and Venice can't handle all the tourists they get every summer. In Florence, where the city's half-million or so inhabitants have to live with the pollution, gridlock, and crime generated by 11 million visitors a year, there's talk not only of boosting hotel taxes, but even of charging admission to some public squares. The idea is to discourage at least some visitors, as well as to pay for cleaning up the mess.

The future

For many poorer countries, tourism may still offer the best hope for development. 'The Vietnamese are doing their best to open up their country,' says Patrick Duffey of the World Tourism Organization. 'Iran is working on a master plan for their tourism. Libya has paid $1 million for a study. They all want tourists. And people like to discover ever new parts of the world, they are tired of mass tourism. Even if a country doesn't have beaches, it can offer mountains and deserts and unique cultures.'

Yet if something isn't done, tourism seems destined to become the victim of its own success. Its impact on the environment is a major concern. In hindsight, tourist organizations might have second thoughts about what exactly they were trying to sell.

As Steve McGuire, a tourist consultant, says, 'Tourism more often than not ruins the very assets it seeks to exploit, and having done the damage, simply moves off elsewhere.'

For poorer countries, tourism may still offer the best hope for development.

Reading

4 Read the title and the quotes in the article. What do you think the article will be about?

5 Read the article. Answer the questions.
1 Which of the places in the pictures on p19 are mentioned?
2 What is said about them?
3 What other places are mentioned?
4 Does the article talk about any of the problems you discussed?
5 The author asks 'What can be done to stop tourism destroying the object of its affection?' What would Steve McGuire's answer be?

6 In groups, discuss these questions.
1 How is tourism destroying the object of its affection in Majorca and the Philippines?
2 What are the statistics of the global tourist industry?
3 What are the effects of tourism?
4 Who are the winners and losers?
5 What are possible future developments?

What do you think?

1 Give your personal reactions to the text using these phrases.

I didn't know/I already knew that ...	What surprised me was ...
It must be really difficult for ...	It's hard to believe that ...
I wonder what can be done to ...	It's a shame that ...

2 In groups, think of more questions to ask the other groups. Use the prompts if you want.

Who ...?	Why ...?	In what way ...?
What is meant by ...?	How many ...?	
What exactly ...?	What are some of the problems ...?	

Who has bought nearly all the property on the island of Majorca?

Vocabulary work

1 Work with a partner. Discuss the meaning of the words highlighted in the article.

2 Match a line in **A** with a line in **B**. Can you remember the contexts?

A	B
the boom	destinations
tourism's vital	venture
per capita	for development
a major business	income
foreign	example
consume	in world travel
a prime	as much water
the best hope	contribution to the economy

SPEAKING AND LISTENING
Dreams come true

1 20,000 people were asked what they most wanted to do before they die. Here are the top fifteen activities.

What are your top five? Number them 1–5. Which ones don't interest you at all? Put an **X**.

- [ ] go whale-watching
- [ ] see the Northern Lights
- [ ] visit Machu Picchu
- [ ] **escape to a paradise island**
- [ ] go white-water rafting
- [ ] fly in a fighter plane
- [ ] **fly in a hot-air balloon**
- [ ] climb Sydney Harbour Bridge
- [ ] swim with dolphins
- [ ] **walk the Great Wall of China**
- [ ] go on safari
- [ ] go skydiving
- [ ] **dive with sharks**
- [ ] drive a Formula 1 car
- [ ] go scuba diving on the Great Barrier Reef

Compare your lists in groups.

2 You can read the actual results of the poll on p91. Does anything surprise you? What do you think is missing from the list?

3 Do you know anyone who has done any of these things? What was it like?

4 **T 2.4** Listen to three people describing their experience of one of these activities. Which one are they talking about? What do they say about it?

VOCABULARY
Hot verbs – *make, do*

1 There are many expressions with *make* and *do*. Look at these examples from the text on p20.

- They wanted ... to *make way* for a holiday resort.
- They aren't *making the connection*.
- The Vietnamese are *doing their best* to open up their country.
- Tourism, having *done the damage*, moves off elsewhere.

2 Put the words in the right box.

| a good impression   business   arrangements   a decision   a difference |
| research   a profit/a loss   your best   a start/a move   sth clear |
| a good job   a degree   an effort   sb a favour   a suggestion |

MAKE	DO

3 Complete the sentences with some of the expressions in exercise 2.

1 When you go for a job interview, it's important to _____ .
2 I think we're all getting tired. Can I _____ ? How about a break?
3 A lot of _____ has been _____ into the causes of cancer.
4 I think the director is basically _____ . He's reliable, he's honest, and he gets results.
5 I'd like to _____ right now that I am totally opposed to this idea.
6 Right. I think we should _____ and get down to business.
7 I don't mind if we go now or later. It _____ no _____ to me.
8 Could you _____ me _____ and lend me some money till tomorrow?

T 2.5 Listen and check.

4 Match an expression in **A** with a line in **B**. Underline the expression with *make* or *do*.

A	B
1 She's made the big time as an actress.	'She's an accountant.'
2 We'll never make the airport in time.	'I can make myself understood.'
3 'What does she do for a living?'	'Yeah. It really made my day.'
4 'You'll all have to do more overtime and work weekends.'	The traffic's too bad.
5 'How much do you want to borrow? £20?'	She can command $20 million a movie.
6 'How much Spanish do you speak?'	'Great. That'll do fine.'
7 'I hear the boss said you'd done really well.'	'That does it! I'm going to look for another job!'

Phrasal verbs

5 Complete the sentences with a phrasal verb with *do*.

| do away with sth   do without sth |
| could do with sth   do sth up |

'I'm tired of wondering what I'd do without you, ... I want to find out for sure.'

1 I'm so thirsty. I _____ a cup of tea.
2 We've bought an old flat. We're going to _____ it _____ over the next few years.
3 I think we should _____ the monarchy. They're all useless. And expensive.
4 I could never _____ my personal assistant. She organizes everything for me.

T 2.6 Listen and check.

6 Do the same with these phrasal verbs with *make*.

| make sth up   make up for sth |
| make sth of sb   make off with sth |

1 Thieves broke into the castle and _____ jewellery and antique paintings.
2 Jake's parents buy him loads of toys. They're trying to _____ always being at work.
3 What do you _____ the new boss? I quite like him.
4 You didn't believe his story, did you? He _____ the whole thing _____ .

T 2.7 Listen and check.

LISTENING AND SPEAKING
Tashi Wheeler – girl on the move

1 What are some of your earliest memories of holidays and travelling as a child? Tell the class, and show any photos you have brought.

2 Look at the photographs of Tashi Wheeler, the daughter of Tony and Maureen (p18). In each photo …
- How old is she?
- Where do you think she is –
  Mexico, Singapore, Kenya (x2), US (Arizona), or Peru?
- What is she doing?

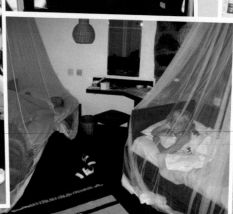

3 Tashi began travelling when she was eight months old. What questions would you like to ask her?

What was the first foreign country you went to?
What are your earliest memories?
Which countries have you been to?

4 **T 2.8** Listen to part one of an interview with Tashi. Does she answer any of your questions?

What memories does she have of …?
- transport
- being on safari
- her mother
- trekking in Nepal

5 **T 2.9** Listen to part two. Correct the wrong information.

> On holiday, the Wheeler family are very relaxed. They get up late and go to bed early. They spend a lot of time on the beach. Tony Wheeler reads the paper. They go to the same restaurant every day. Tashi and her brother spend a lot of time watching movies. She doesn't feel that travel broadens the mind.

6 **T 2.10** Listen to part three and answer the questions.
1. How did her attitude to travel change as she got older?
2. What did she find difficult socially?
3. Why was 'adjusting back and forth' difficult?
4. What did the kids at school have that she didn't? What did she have that they didn't?
5. Where does she feel comfortable? Where does she feel uncomfortable?
6. What are Tashi's final bits of advice for future travellers?
7. 'I get very itchy-footed.' Which phrase with a similar meaning did Tommy Willis use on p17?

SPOKEN ENGLISH Fillers

When we speak (in any language!), we can be vague and imprecise. We also use fillers, which don't mean very much, but fill the gaps!

Tashi	And Galapagos Islands, Philippines, *and stuff like that.* … monkeys swinging off the rear-view mirrors, *and things.* The getting up at *like* four in the morning …
Interviewer	And when you were on these travels, *I mean*, did your dad *sort of* have a notebook, and he'd be *sort of* stopping everywhere …?

Look at the tapescript on p72. Find more examples of imprecise language and fillers.

EVERYDAY ENGLISH
Exclamations

1 Look at these examples of exclamations. When do we use *What a(n) …!, What …!,* and *How…!*?

What an exciting experience!   What nonsense!   How horrible!

2 Match an exclamation in **B** with a line in **C**.

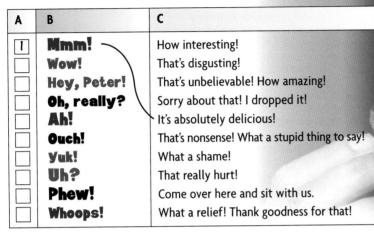

A	B	C
1	**Mmm!**	How interesting!
	Wow!	That's disgusting!
	Hey, Peter!	That's unbelievable! How amazing!
	Oh, really?	Sorry about that! I dropped it!
	Ah!	It's absolutely delicious!
	Ouch!	That's nonsense! What a stupid thing to say!
	Yuk!	What a shame!
	Uh?	That really hurt!
	Phew!	Come over here and sit with us.
	Whoops!	What a relief! Thank goodness for that!

3 **T 2.11** Listen to ten lines of conversation. Reply to each one using an exclamation in **B** and its matching line in **C**. Write the number of the conversation 1–10 in column **A**.

4 What is the next line in each conversation? Put a number 1–10 next to the correct line.

> **A** How's your steak? Is it OK?
> **B** Mmm! It's absolutely delicious! **Just the way I like it.**

☐	Don't worry. I'll get you a new one.
☐	Triplets! That'll keep them busy!
☐	You must be so disappointed!
1	Just the way I like it.
☐	I hadn't done any revising for it at all.
☐	You wouldn't catch me eating that!
☐	I told you! Well, it isn't bleeding, but you'll have a nice bruise.
☐	Let's have a chat.
☐	You know it's not true.
☐	I haven't seen her for ages. How is she?

T 2.12 Listen and check. Practise the conversations, paying special attention to intonation. You could act some of them out and make them longer!

Music of English 🎵♩

With exclamations using *What …!* and *How …!*, your intonation should rise and fall on both the adjective and noun:

⌢⌢ ⌢⌢   ⌢⌢ ⌢⌢   ⌢⌢
What awful shoes!   *What a fantastic view!*   *How amazing!*

T 2.13 Listen and repeat.

---

5 Put *What …, What a …,* or *How …* to complete the exclamations.

1 _____ silly mistake!
2 _____ brilliant idea!
3 _____ utterly ridiculous!
4 _____ dreadful weather!
5 _____ rubbish!
6 _____ mess!
7 _____ awful!
8 _____ wonderful!
9 _____ relief!
10 _____ terrible thing to happen!

Which are positive reactions? Which are negative?

6 **T 2.14** Listen to some situations. Respond to them, using one of the exclamations in exercise 5.

7 Write a dialogue with a partner. Use some of the exclamations on this page. You could ask about a party, a meal, a holiday, or a sports event.

Begin with a question.

> **What was the … like?**
> **Well, it was …**

Act out your conversations to the class.

3 What a story!

TEST YOUR GRAMMAR

Read the story. Put the events into chronological order. What happened first? What happened last?

Burglar arrested

▶ A COUPLE came home at midnight to find their house had been burgled. Bob and Janet Gilbreath had left their house at six o'clock to go to the theatre. When they got home, the back door had been smashed, and money and jewellery stolen. A neighbour said that she had heard a loud noise at about eight o'clock. Mr and Mrs Gilbreath, who moved to the house five years ago, told police that they had seen a man who had been acting suspiciously for several days before the robbery, and were able to give a description. A man answering the description was later arrested.

WHAT'S IN THE NEWS?

Narrative tenses

1 Look at the newspaper headlines. What do you think is the whole story?

2 What would you like to know? Write some more questions.

   Did he mean to fall over?
   Where was she climbing?
   How did he manage to hack into their systems?

3 **T 3.1** Listen to three conversations about the stories. Which of your questions were answered?

4 Here are the answers to some questions. What are the questions?

   1 Just ordinary clothes.
   2 For a dare.
   3 Three hours.
   4 In a shelter.
   5 His own software program.
   6 To download from the Internet.

5 Match lines in **A** and **B**. Practise saying them with contracted and weak forms.

A	B
He was wearing	with a partner.
He'd been talking	he wouldn't do it.
His friends had bet him	the next night.
She was climbing	about doing it for ages.
They were rescued	ordinary clothes.

T 3.2 Listen and check.

Man survives plunge over Niagara Falls

180ft drop

Climber saved by

From: Rachel
Need heli rescue off
north ridge of piz Bad
ile. Switzerland

The nerd who hacked into US Defence systems

text plea to friend

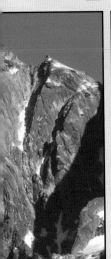

1 Complete the chart using the verb in brackets.

Past Simple	Past Continuous
(fall)	(read)
Past Perfect	**Past Perfect Continuous**
(hear)	(act)
Past Simple passive	**Past Perfect passive**
(arrest)	(burgle)

Look at tapescript T 3.1 on p73. Find an example of each tense. When do we use the Past Perfect? When do we use continuous tenses?

2 Why are different tenses used in these paragraphs?

John cooked a lovely meal. His guests had a good time. They left at midnight.

Just after midnight, John was looking at the mess. His guests had just left. He'd cooked a lovely meal, and everyone had had a good time.

▶▶ **Grammar Reference pp82–83**

PRACTICE

Discussing grammar

1 Compare the use of tenses in these sentences. Say which tense is used and why.

1	I read I was reading	a book on the plane.

2	When Alice arrived,	I made a cake. I was making a cake. I had made a cake.

3	The film started The film had started	when we got to the cinema.

4	He was sacked because	he had stolen some money. he had been stealing money for years.

5	When I got to the garage, my car	was being repaired. had been repaired.

UXBRIDGE COLLEGE
LEARNING CENTRE

Writing narratives

2 Rewrite the sentences as one sentence, beginning with the part in **bold**.

She won £2,000 in a competition. **Last night Sally was celebrating.**
Last night Sally was celebrating because she'd won £2,000 in a competition.

1 He got up at dawn. He was driving for ten hours. **Peter was tired when he arrived home.**
2 I parked my car on a yellow line. It was towed away. **I went to get my car, but it wasn't there.** (*When ...*)
3 He wasn't always poor. He had a successful business. Unfortunately, it went bust. **Mick was a homeless beggar.**
4 They were shopping all day. They spent all their money on clothes. **Jane and Peter arrived home.** They were broke. (*When ...*)
5 He saw a house in Scotland. He first saw it while he was driving on holiday. **Last week John moved to the house.**

The news

3 **T 3.3** Listen to the first story. Correct the mistakes in the sentences.

1 Ten workers have died.
2 They'd been trapped up a mountain.
3 They'd been building a new road.
4 There was an avalanche.
5 Sixteen men managed to escape.
6 Ten were fatally injured.
7 The men were recovering at home.
8 The cause of the accident is known.

4 **T 3.4** Listen to the second news item. Here are the answers to some questions. Write the questions.

1 For two days.
2 After school on Wednesday.
3 Their photographs.
4 Nearby houses.
5 A neighbour.
6 In a garden shed.
7 No, they hadn't. (*... realized ...?*)

SPOKEN ENGLISH   News and responses

When we tell a story, we use certain expressions. When we listen to a story, we respond with different expressions. Put **G** (giving news), **R** (reacting to news), or **A** (asking for more information) after each expression.

1 ☐ Did you read that story about ... ?
2 ☐ What happened to him?
3 ☐ That's amazing!
4 ☐ What did he do it for?
5 ☐ Apparently ...
6 ☐ What a crazy guy!
7 ☐ You're kidding!
8 ☐ Then what happened?
9 ☐ Actually, ...
10 ☐ I don't get it.

Work with a partner. You are going to read and discuss two news stories.

Student A Read the story on p91.
Student B Read the story on p92.

When you've read your story, tell your partner about it. Try to use some of the phrases for giving and responding to news.

▶▶ **WRITING** Narrative writing 1 – Using adverbs in narratives *p65*

VOCABULARY AND SPEAKING
Books and films

1 We usually want to know some things about a book before we start reading it. Here are some answers. Write in the questions.

1 <u>Who wrote it</u>_____?
Charles Dickens/Jane Austen.

2 _____?
It's a romantic novel/It's a thriller/It's a biography.

3 _____?
It's about a tragic marriage/It's about politics and corruption.

4 <u>Where and</u>_____?
In India in the last century/In New York in the 80s.

5 _____?
A lawyer called Potts and his client, Lady Jane /A detective called Blunket.

6 _____?
Yes, it has. It came out quite a few years ago and starred Johnny Depp.

7 _____?
It ends really tragically/It's frustrating because we don't really know/They all live happily ever after.

8 _____?
I thought it was great/I couldn't put it down/I didn't want it to end/It was OK but I skipped the boring bits.

9 _____?
Yes, I would. It's great if you like a good love story/It's a terrific holiday read.

2 Which questions could also be asked about a film? Some might have to change. What extra questions can be asked about a film?

3 **T 3.5** Listen to two people, one talking about a film and the other a book. Take notes under these headings.

Title	Setting	Characters	Plot	Personal opinion

4 Work with a partner. Ask and answer the questions in exercise 1 about your favourite book or film.

5 Look at the front and back covers of *The Blind Assassin*. Which of the questions in exercise 1 can you answer?

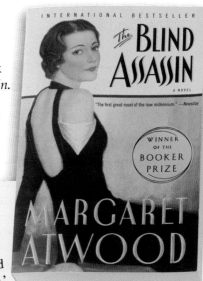

INTERNATIONAL BESTSELLER

The **BLIND ASSASSIN**
A NOVEL

"The first great novel of the new millennium." —*Newsday*

WINNER OF THE BOOKER PRIZE

MARGARET ATWOOD

FICTION/LITERATURE

'Grand storytelling on a grand scale . . . . Sheerly enjoyable.'
The Washington Post Book World

The Booker Prize-winning sensation from the incomparable Margaret Atwood— a novel that combines elements of gothic drama, romantic suspense, and science fiction fantasy in a spellbinding narrative. *The Blind Assassin* opens with these simple resonant words: "Ten days after the war ended, my sister Laura drove a car off a bridge." They are spoken by Iris Chase Griffen, sole surviving descendant of a once rich and influential Ontario family, whose terse account of her sister's death in 1945 is followed by an inquest report proclaiming the death accidental. But just as the reader expects to settle into Laura's story, Atwood introduces a novel-within-a-novel. Entitled *The Blind Assassin*, it is a science fiction story improvised by two unnamed lovers who meet in dingy backstreet rooms. When we return to Iris, it is through a 1947 newspaper article announcing the discovery of a sailboat carrying the dead body of her husband, a distinguished industrialist.

What makes this novel Margaret Atwood's strongest and most profoundly entertaining is the way in which the three wonderfully rich stories weave together, gradually revealing through their interplay the secrets surrounding the entire Chase family – and most particularly the fascinating and tangled lives of the two sisters. *The Blind Assassin* is a brilliant and enthralling book by a writer at the top of her form.

'Absorbing….Expertly rendered….Virtuosic storytelling.'
The New York Times

$14.95

ISBN 0-385-72095-5
51495
9 780385 720953

Cover illustration: Courtesy of the Advertising Archive, London
© The Curtis Publishing Co.
Cover design: Mario J. Pulice
Hand lettering: Anita Karl

READING GROUP GUIDE AVAILABLE AT
www.anchorbooks.com

READING AND SPEAKING
The Blind Assassin

1 Read the first part of *The Blind Assassin*. Which two words would you like your teacher to explain? Which statement do you agree with?

- The facts are presented coldly and clinically.
- The violence of the accident is described with great emotion.

2 Read the second part. Answer the questions.

1 Who are Laura, Richard, Mrs Griffen, and Alex? How are they related? (The narrator's name is Iris.)
2 What are the various suggested causes of the crash? How does Iris explain the crash to the policeman? Does she really believe this?
3 Why is she angry with her sister?

3 Read the final part. Answer the questions.

1 Why is Iris wondering what clothes to wear?
2 What impression do you have of her and her background?
3 Who is Reenie? What do we learn about the mother of Iris and Laura?
4 Who do you think the last line refers to?

4 When is Iris ...?

- calm
- nostalgic
- very angry
- clear thinking
- cold and factual

What evidence is there that Laura ...?

- didn't care about people's feelings
- felt guilty about something
- had bad experiences in life
- had suffered even as a child

Language work

1 The writer uses many dramatic words. Match a word from the extract with a more neutral description.

charred	turning and twisting
smithereens	things people do
plunged	knocking together (teeth)
swirling	making a loud cry (in pain)
suspended	very small pieces
chattering	lift quickly
deeds	badly burnt
scoop	fell suddenly downwards
howling	hung

What do you think?

1 The first chapter of this novel raises more questions than it answers. What has the author *not* told us? What do you want to know?

2 Which do you think is true?

- Laura's notebooks are ... her childhood diaries/a record of a secret relationship/a novel.
- Laura suffered because ... she was mentally ill/her mother died/she had an unhappy love life.
- Iris ... feels responsible for her sister's death/never loved her husband.

CHAPTER I
The bridge

Ten days after the war ended, my sister Laura drove a car off a bridge. The bridge was being repaired: she went right through the Danger sign. The car fell a hundred feet into the ravine, smashing through the treetops feathery with new leaves, then burst into flames and rolled down into the shallow creek at the bottom. Chunks of the bridge fell on top of it. Nothing much was left of her but charred smithereens.

I was informed of the accident by a policeman: the car was mine, and they'd traced the licence. His tone was respectful: no doubt he recognized Richard's name. He said the tires may have caught on a streetcar track or the brakes may have failed, but he also felt bound to inform me that two witnesses – a retired lawyer and a bank teller, dependable people – had claimed to have seen the whole thing. They'd said Laura had turned the car sharply and deliberately, and had plunged off the bridge with no more fuss than stepping off a curb. They'd noticed her hands on the wheel because of the white gloves she'd been wearing.

It wasn't the brakes, I thought. She had her reasons. Not that they were ever the same as anybody else's reasons. She was completely ruthless in that way.

'I suppose you want someone to identify her,' I said. 'I'll come down as soon as I can.' I could hear the calmness of my own voice, as if from a distance. In reality I could barely get the words out; my mouth was numb, my entire face was rigid with pain. I felt as if I'd been to the dentist. I was furious with Laura for what she'd done, but also with the policeman for implying that she'd done it. A hot wind was blowing around my head, the strands of my hair lifting and swirling in it, like ink spilled in water.

'I'm afraid there will be an inquest, Mrs. Griffen,' he said.

'Naturally,' I said. 'But it was an accident. My sister was never a good driver.'

I could picture the smooth oval of Laura's face, her neatly pinned chignon, the dress she would have been wearing: a blue or steel grey or hospital-corridor green. Penitential colours – less like something she'd chosen to put on than like something she'd been locked up in. Her solemn half-smile; the amazed lift of her eyebrows, as if she were admiring the view.

The white gloves: a Pontius Pilate gesture. She was washing her hands of me. Of all of us.

What had she been thinking of as the car sailed off the bridge, then hung suspended in the afternoon sunlight, glinting like a dragonfly for that one instant of held breath before the plummet? Of Alex, of Richard, of bad faith, of our father and his wreckage: of God, perhaps, and her fatal triangular bargain. Or of the stack of cheap school exercise books that she must have hidden that very morning, in the bureau drawer where I kept my stockings, knowing I would be the one to find them.

When the policeman had gone I went upstairs to change. To visit the morgue I would need gloves, and a hat with a veil. Something to cover the eyes. There might be reporters. I would have to call a taxi. Also I ought to warn Richard, at his office: he would wish to have a statement of grief prepared. I went into my dressing room: I would need black, and a handkerchief.

I opened the drawer, I saw the notebooks. I undid the criss-cross of kitchen string that tied them together. I noticed that my teeth were chattering, and that I was cold all over. I must be in shock, I decided.

What I remembered then was Reenie, from when we were little. It was Reenie who'd done the bandaging, of scrapes and cuts and minor injuries: Mother might be resting, or doing good deeds elsewhere, but Reenie was always there. She'd scoop us up and sit us on the white enamel kitchen table, alongside the pie dough she was rolling out or the chicken she was cutting up or the fish she was gutting, and give us a lump of brown sugar to get us to close our mouths. *Tell me where it hurts*, she'd say. *Stop howling. Just calm down and show me where.*

But some people can't tell where it hurts. They can't calm down. They can't ever stop howling.

LISTENING AND SPEAKING
The money jigsaw

Our **£2,000** jigsaw

1 Look at the headlines and photographs. With a partner, use the prompts to invent the story.

> walking to school / ripped up bank notes / flying all over / a bin / a plastic bag / jammed full / torn up notes / had to go to school

> after school playing / police / told them where / police took away / Bank of England / long time / gave back / stick together

Stick-up job on torn bank notes leaves schoolgirls £1,200 richer

What do you think?

Why do you think someone tore up the money? Rachel and her friend have two theories.

- Maybe an old lady decided she wasn't going to leave it to anyone.
- It could have been a divorce – one person didn't want the other to have it.

Do you agree? Do you have any better explanations?

2 **T 3.6** Listen to one of the girls, Rachel Aumann, being interviewed. Compare your story with hers. (*Sainsbury's* is the name of a supermarket.)

3 Answer the questions.

1 Where did the girls find the money?
2 How big are the pieces?
3 Are they being allowed to keep it?
4 Is it easy to stick the notes together?
5 How do they do it?
6 How long have they been doing it?
7 How much money is there?

SPOKEN ENGLISH *like*

Rachel uses the word *like* a lot.

> Yeah, it was ... erm ... like really out of the ordinary. ... we traced it to like a bin.

This use of *like* suggests that the speaker (often a younger person) is not making an effort to be precise when describing or reporting a situation.

Look at the tapescript on p73. Find more examples of *like*. Which example shows the correct use of *like* as a preposition?

EVERYDAY ENGLISH
Showing interest and surprise

1 **T 3.7** Listen to the dialogue. Write in **B**'s answers. How does she show interest and surprise?

A Jade's got a new boyfriend.
B _____? Good for her!
A Apparently, he lives in a castle.
B _____? How amazing!
A Yes. She met him in Slovenia.
B _____? That's interesting.
A Unfortunately, he can't speak much English.
B _____? I thought everyone could these days!

2 **B** uses *echo questions* and *reply questions*. Which are which? Practise the conversation with your partner. Pay particular attention to the stress and intonation.

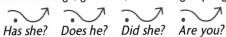

To show interest, the intonation on echo and reply questions should start high, go down, and then go up high at the end.

Has she?   Does he?   Did she?   Are you?

T 3.8 Listen and repeat.

If you use these short questions without any intonation, you will sound bored and uninterested!

3 Complete the conversations with either an echo or a reply question.

1 **A** Sam wants to apologize.
   B _____?
   A Yes. He's broken your mother's Chinese vase.
   B _____? Oh, no!

2 **A** We had a terrible holiday.
   B _____?
   A Yes. It rained all the time.
   B _____?
   A Yes. And the food was disgusting!
   B _____? What a drag!

3 **A** I'm broke.
   B _____? How come?
   A Because I just had a phone bill for £500.
   B _____? Why so much?
   A Because I have a girlfriend in Korea.
   B _____? How interesting!

4 **A** It took me three hours to get here.
   B _____?
   A Yes. There was a traffic jam ten miles long.
   B _____? That's awful!
   A Now I've got a headache!
   B _____? Poor darling. I'll get you something for it.

5 **A** I'm on a mountain, watching the sun set.
   B _____?
   A Yes. And I've got something very important to ask you.
   B _____? What is it? I can't wait!
   A You'd better sit down. I'd like to marry you.
   B _____? Wow!

T 3.9 Listen and compare. Practise them with a partner.

4 Your teacher will read out some sentences about himself/herself. Respond, using a reply question or an echo.

4 Nothing but the truth

Questions and negatives · Prefixes and antonyms · Being polite

TEST YOUR GRAMMAR

1 Make the sentences negative. Sometimes there is more than one possibility.

> *I disagree/don't agree with you.*

1 I agree with you.
2 I think you're right.
3 I told her to go home.
4 'Is John coming?' 'I hope so.'
5 I knew everybody at the party.
6 I've already done my homework.
7 You must get a visa.
8 My sister likes hip-hop, too.

2 Write in the missing word in each question.

1 'What ___ of music do you like?' 'Jazz.'
2 'How ___ do you wash your hair?' 'Every other day.'
3 'Who do you look ___?' 'My mother.'
4 'How ___ does it take you to get to school?' 'Nearly an hour.'
5 'What were you talking to the teacher ___?' 'Oh, this and that.'
6 'Do you know what the time ___?' 'Just after three.'

Ask and answer the questions with a partner.

TELLING LIES
Questions and negatives

1 Think of some lies that these people might tell.

> a teenage girl to her parents   a car salesman
> a student to the teacher   a politician
> a husband to his wife

2 All the people in the cartoons are lying. Who to? Why?

3 ▮ **T 4.1** ▮ Listen to what the people are really thinking. What *is* the truth? Why *did* they lie? Do you think any of the people have good reasons to lie?

4 Which question was each person asked before they lied? Put *a–f* in the boxes.

1 ☐ What did you make that face for? Doesn't it look good?
2 ☐ Can I speak to Sue Jones, please? It's urgent.
3 ☐ How come you're ill today? You looked just fine yesterday!
4 ☐ Who gave you that black eye? Haven't I told you not to get into fights?
5 ☐ Where are you going? How long will you be? I hope you won't be late.
6 ☐ I want to know if you'll marry me. I don't think you will.

a

SORRY CRAIG. IT'S NOT THAT I DON'T LOVE YOU. IT'S JUST THAT I'M NOT READY FOR MARRIAGE YET.

b

NOBODY HIT ME. I FELL DOWN IN THE SCHOOL PLAYGROUND.

1 In exercise 4, find and read aloud …

Questions

… questions with auxiliary verbs.
… questions without auxiliary verbs.
… two ways of asking *Why?*
… a question with a preposition at the end.
… a question word + an adverb.
… an indirect question.

Negatives

… negative questions.
… a future negative.
… negatives with *think* and *hope*.

2 Indirect questions

Make these direct questions indirect using the expressions.

Where does he work? I don't know …
What's the answer? Have you any idea … ?
Did she buy the blue one? I wonder …

▶▶▶ **Grammar Reference pp83–84**

PRACTICE

Quiztime!

1 Work in two groups. You are going to write some questions for a general knowledge quiz.

Group A Look at the information on p91.
Group B Look at the information on p92.

Write the questions for your quiz in your group. Ask and answer questions between groups.

2 Make comments about the answers in the quiz. Some of your sentences might be indirect questions.

We weren't sure …

We didn't have a clue …

We had no idea …

None of us knew …

We guessed …

Did you all know … ?

… how many legs a butterfly has.

… which theory Charles Darwin developed.

Asking for more information

3 We can respond to a statement with a short question to ask for more information.

I went out for a meal last night. — Who with?

My aunt sent me a postcard. — Where from?

Write short questions with a preposition to answer these statements.

1 She gave away all her money.
2 Can I have a word with you, please?
3 I danced all night.
4 I need £5,000 urgently.
5 I got a lovely present today.
6 I bought a birthday card today.
7 Sh! I'm thinking!
8 Do you think you could give me a lift?

4 Make the short questions into longer ones.

Who did you go out for a meal with?   Where did she send it from?

T 4.2 Listen and check your answers. Notice that all the questions end with the preposition.

Negative questions

5 **T 4.3** Listen and compare the use of negative questions in 1 and 2.

1 a Don't you like pizza? How unusual!
  b Can't you swim? I thought everybody learned to at school these days!
  c Hasn't the postman been yet? It's nearly midday!

2 a Haven't we met somewhere before? Wasn't it in Paris?
  b Wasn't it your birthday last week? Sorry I forgot.
  c Isn't that Hugh Grant over there? You know, the actor! I'm sure it is!

In which group …?

… does the speaker ask for confirmation of what he thinks is true and expect the answer *Yes*?

… does the speaker express surprise and expect the answer *No*?

T 4.3 Practise the negative questions. Pay attention to stress and intonation.

6 Give answers to the negative questions in exercise 5.

1 a **No, I've never liked pizza. Can't stand it, I'm afraid.**
2 a **Yes, that's right. It was at the sales conference in La Défense.**

7 Ask and answer about these things using negative questions.

Expressing surprise
like   ice-cream/learning English/your neighbours?
have   ever been abroad/got a TV at home?

Asking for confirmation
is   it Tuesday today/this your pen?
go   to the States last year/to the races next weekend?

T 4.4 Listen and compare.

Making negatives

8 Make a negative sentence about these people. Use your dictionary.

Vegans don't eat any animal products.

vegans atheists teetotallers insomniacs dyslexics pacifists animal rights campaigners naturists anti-globalization protesters

9 **T 4.5** Listen to the first part of a description of a man called Norman. Which words in exercise 8 describe him? Make some negative sentences about him.

He can't sleep.   **He doesn't have a big place to live.**

SPOKEN ENGLISH *How come?* *How come?* can be used instead of *Why?* in informal spoken English. However, they are not the same. Look at these sentences. Which question expresses surprise? *Why are you learning English?* *How come you're going to work today? It's Sunday.* Note that *How come?* is not followed by the usual inverted word order of question forms.

10 **T 4.5** Listen to the second part of the description of Norman. There are lots of contradictions. Complete the sentences about Norman below with a question using *How come?*

My mate Norman

He lives in a tiny one-roomed flat so **how come he came downstairs to the living room?**
He's an insomniac, so **how come he slept so well?**
He's single, so …
He hasn't got any pets, so …
He's an atheist, so …
He's dyslexic, so …
He's unemployed, so …
He's teetotal, so …
He's vegetarian, so …
He's anti-social, so …

Who is it?

11 Write a description of yourself using *only* negative sentences. Your teacher will distribute them amongst the students in the class. Read them aloud and guess who it is.

I can't cook.   **I never arrive on time.**
I didn't pass the test last week.

LISTENING AND SPEAKING
My most memorable lie!

Work in small groups.

1 Did you ever tell lies as a child? Can you remember any? Talk about them in your groups. Decide which is the most interesting lie in your group and tell the class.

2 **T 4.6** Listen to six people talking about their most memorable lie. Correct the statements.

1 **Andrew** was playing in the swimming pool when his father came home.

2 **Paul** only lied once as a child because he swore and stole biscuits.

3 **Carolyn** went to America for her girlfriend's wedding.

4 **Kiki** finally told her grandmother the truth.

5 **Sean** learnt Judo at school.

6 **Kate** was not punished for lying.

3 Listen again and answer the questions.

1 Andrew says, *I completely denied all knowledge.* Of what? How had he tried to hide the evidence?

2 Paul says, *bizarrely what you end up doing is lying ... so that you've got something to say.* Lying to who? When? Why is it bizarre?

3 Carolyn says, *I had to tell a white lie.* What was it? Why was it a white lie? What *did nothing* for whose figure?

4 Kiki says, *I know where I lost it.* What did she lose? Where did she lose it? What was her lie?

5 Sean says, *somebody's mother rang my mother to get details.* To get details of what? Why did he lie in the first place?

6 Kate says, *I put him in the box ... and I shut the lid.* Who did she put in the box? Which box? How does she excuse her behaviour?

4 Which words go with which lie? What do they refer to?

confession	frumpy	dressing up box	gold-filtered
a robbery	spanked	stubs necklace	the playground
a princess	a grate	a soldier	sins

What do you think?

- Which of the six lies do you think are 'good' reasons to lie? Which are 'bad'? Which are 'white lies'?

- Work alone. List other occasions when you think it might be good to lie and occasions when it is definitely not.

- Discuss your ideas with your group. Do you all agree about what are 'good' and 'bad' lies?

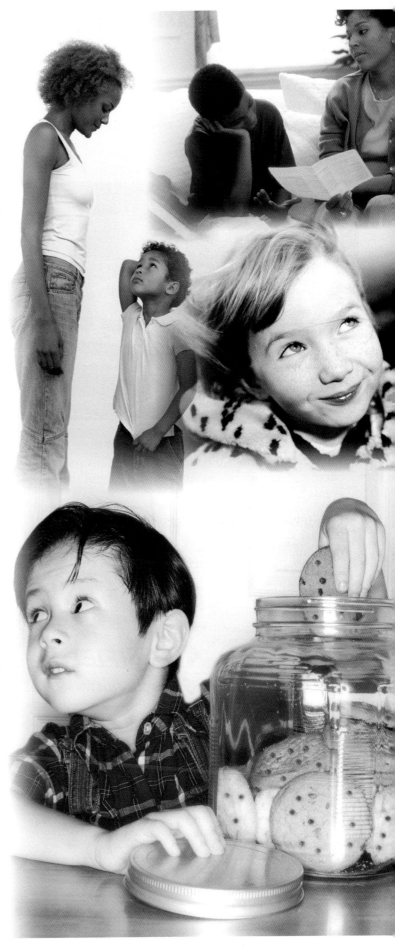

READING AND SPEAKING
Diana and Elvis shot JFK!

1 What do you know about the following events? Discuss in groups and share information.
- The deaths of President John F. Kennedy, John Lennon, Elvis Presley, Princess Diana.
- The Apollo moon landings.

2 There are many conspiracy theories about these events. What are conspiracy theories? How are they usually circulated nowadays? Do you know any about the events in exercise 1?

3 Read the introduction to three of the world's most popular conspiracy theories. Which events are mentioned? Why do people like these theories? What is a 'juicy' theory?

CLASSIFIED

EVERYBODY loves a good conspiracy theory. Whether it is the CIA shooting President Kennedy, or Elvis being alive and well and living on the Moon, there are few things that appeal to the imagination more than a mixture of mystery and a hint of evil-doing in high places. When horrifying, historic events shake our world we seek to make sense of them by creating bizarre theories. These theories, however unlikely, are preferable to the cold fact that sometimes accidents happen. Many of the juiciest theories circulate on the Internet.

4 Work in groups of three.

Student A Read the article on p39.
Student B Read the article on p40.
Student C Read the article on p41.

Answer the questions.

1 When and what was the event?
2 How many theories are mentioned? Write a list of the different ones in note form.
3 What proof is given to support them?
4 What reasons are suggested for hiding the true facts?
5 Which people, individual or groups, are mentioned in relation to the event?

Compare your answers with the others in your group.

Vocabulary work

Find words in your text to replace those in *italics*. Explain them to the others in your group.

Diana
1 The huge number of websites is *absolutely amazing*.
2 The florists *devised* a *clever but wicked* plot to murder Diana.
3 The car crash was a *carefully planned trick*.
4 I don't *believe* any of these theories.
5 Someone in the royal family *devised* a plot to *interfere* with the brakes.

Moon landing
1 Rumours have been *going round* for many years.
2 The US flag is seen *blowing* and there is no *wind* on the moon.
3 A *fantastic exhibition* of stars.
4 Scientists have *all* agreed that the theorists don't have *any argument at all*.
5 NASA has been desperately *trying to hide* evidence of life.

JFK Junior
1 There are many *strange* theories – one of the *craziest* claims he was murdered by Clinton supporters.
2 Explosives were *stuck* to the tail of the plane.
3 The plane *hit violent air movements*.
4 The crash happened *strangely and coincidentally* on the 30th anniversary.
5 Some explanations are *clearly stupid*. Others are *quite believable*.

What do you think?

- Which theories are the most believable/unbelievable?
- What is it about the Internet that breeds such theories?
- Think of a recent major news event and work in your groups to devise conspiracy theories about it. Describe the event and your theories to the class.

 WRITING Linking ideas – Conjunctions **p66**

CONSPIRACY THEORY 1   THE DEATH OF DIANA

The first Diana conspiracy site appeared on the Internet in Australia only hours after her death on August 31st, 1997. Since then an estimated 36,000 Diana conspiracy websites have been set up – breathtaking by anyone's standards. Hypotheses range from pure James Bond ('it was all an MI6 plot to protect the monarchy') to farce ('it was a fiendish murder plot thought up by the world's florists to sell lots of flowers'). And most popular of all, Diana, Princess of Wales, isn't dead after all – that terrible car crash in Paris was an elaborate hoax to enable the Princess and her boyfriend, Dodi Fayed, to fake their own deaths so that they could live in blissful isolation for the rest of their lives. Subscribers to this theory say that Diana was fed up with the intrusions into her private life and used the wealth and resources of the Fayed family to fake her death, and now she and Dodi are living on a small tropical island, communicating with her sons by satellite video conferencing. Think about it, they say, we never actually saw her body, did we?

> 'We never actually saw her body, did we?'

You don't buy into any of these theories? Don't worry. There are plenty more to choose from. For example, Paul Burrell, Diana's former butler, claims that the Princess predicted her own death in a car crash. Apparently, she was so frightened that ten months before her death she wrote to Burrell saying that a plot was being hatched by a member of the royal family and that her car's brakes would be tampered with and she would suffer serious head injuries. And all of this so that the Prince of Wales could marry again.

These theories multiply because it is so hard for us to believe that a princess, with all her wealth and bodyguards, could be killed by something as arbitrary and mundane as a traffic accident. Psychologically, we need conspiracy theories to make the tragedies of life more bearable. And the Internet helps feed the global paranoia.

CONSPIRACY THEORY 2

THE APOLLO MOON LANDING

For over 30 years rumours have been circulating that the Apollo Moon landings were faked. They say astronaut Neil Armstrong made no 'giant leap for mankind', they assert that the 1969 Moon mission was a hoax to prove America won the space race, that the astronauts were 'astro-nots'! The high point in the Great Moon Landing Conspiracy came on 15 February 2001, the date that the Fox television network broadcast a programme entitled Did We Land on the Moon? This alleged that the whole Moon landing had been staged inside a film studio on a US military base somewhere in the Mojave desert.

The programme claimed:

1 The US flag planted on the Moon's surface is seen fluttering, and there is no breeze of any kind on the Moon.
2 The photographs taken by the astronauts do not include any of the Moon's night sky, where there would have been a stunning array of stars on view.
3 The shadows in the pictures are clearly coming from more than one angle – an impossibility on the Moon, where the only light source is the Sun, but more than plausible inside a film studio.
4 One of the famed Moon rocks brought back by the Apollo astronauts is marked with a telltale letter 'C', suggesting the markings not of some alien life force but of a film prop.

'Was the whole moon landing staged inside a film studio?'

After the programme the Internet went crazy with theories and counter-theories. However, scientists have unanimously agreed that the conspiracy theorists don't have even the beginnings of a case. Too many things about the Apollo missions were impossible to fake, from the radio signals picked up at listening stations around the world, to the Moon rocks, which have been subjected to repeated geological analysis and clearly date back several millennia.

Finally there are the UFO 'nuts'. They actually do believe that astronauts went to the Moon, and found not only a load of rocks, but also widespread evidence of an ancient alien civilization — a discovery so terrifying that NASA has been desperately seeking to conceal it from the public ever since.

Moon rock

CONSPIRACY THEORY 3

THE DEATH OF JOHN F KENNEDY JR.

John Kennedy Junior, son of assassinated US president JFK, was killed on July 17th 1999 when his tiny Piper Saratoga aircraft crashed over Martha's Vineyard, near Boston. He was piloting the plane on the way to a family wedding with his wife Carolyn. To millions of Americans, JFK Junior was the closest thing to royalty the United States has ever had, and, as with his father, with every anniversary of his death they come up with ever more bizarre conspiracy theories to explain the tragedy.

One of the wildest theories claims that Kennedy Junior, known as 'John John', was murdered by Clinton supporters because he planned to stand against Hillary Clinton in the New York senate race.

Another theory asserts that an explosion, heard over Martha's Vineyard at the time of the crash, suggests that terrorists placed a bomb on the tiny plane. It is claimed that leaked FBI documents record the discovery of explosives glued within its tail.

> 'Some of the explanations for the plane crash are patently ridiculous.'

A third theory blames Kennedy's beautiful blonde wife, Carolyn. It is suggested that she caused the crash by chatting on her mobile phone just as the plane ran into turbulence over Martha's Vineyard, thus interfering with the controls while her husband was desperately trying to make an emergency landing. However, the most popular theory of all blames the crash on the legendary Irish curse said to have taken the lives of so many of the Kennedy clan. This curse, reputed to have followed the Kennedy dynasty over from Ireland, is said to strike when Kennedy members are around water. John John's uncle Joseph Kennedy Jr. died in a flight over water during World War II, while another uncle, Teddy Kennedy, drove off a bridge into water at Chappaquiddick – spookily, the plane crash happened on the 30th anniversary of the Chappaquiddick incident.

'Some of the explanations for the plane crash are patently ridiculous,' says a Kennedy watcher. 'Others like the cell phone theory are based on recorded information and are pretty plausible.'

VOCABULARY
Saying the opposite

1 What part of speech are these words? Write antonyms for them using prefixes if possible.

Word	Antonym(s)
fake adj	genuine, real, authentic
like vb	dislike, hate, can't stand
tiny	
happiness	
guilty	
safe	
admit	
sincere	
success	
mature	
encourage	
kind/generous	
appear	

⊘ UP
⊘ UNDECIDED
⊘ DOWN

BEWLEY

2 Complete the conversations with antonyms from the box. Put the words in the correct form.

improve   safety   success   criticize   generosity
fail   mean   encourage   get worse   danger

1 **A** Gary's a really _____ businessman.
  B Yeah, but he's a complete _____ as a family man. He never sees his children.

2 **A** My grandad's so _____, he gives me £20 every time I see him.
  B Lucky you. My grandad's famous for his _____. A fiver every birthday, if he remembers.

3 **A** Well, Henry, I'm pleased there's been some _____ in your behaviour this term, but sadly your work has _____.
  B Didn't I do OK in the test then?

4 **A** You're not going bungee jumping! It sounds really _____.
  B No, honestly, it's _____ enough as long as you're careful.

5 **A** Our teacher is always _____ us. I feel useless.
  B I know – it's not fair, he should give us more _____ if he wants us to work hard.

T 4.7 Listen and check.

3 What is the effect of using antonyms in these conversations?

A What **lousy** weather!
B Yes, it's not exactly **tropical**, is it?

A Jenny's **thick**, isn't she?
B Well, she isn't the **brightest of people**, it's true.

Write similar conversations with a partner about these topics. How could you describe the following both honestly and tactfully?
• a boring party   • an awful holiday   • a mean friend   • a difficult exam

T 4.8 Listen and compare.

4 What's the opposite of ... ?

1 a tough question   3 fair hair   5 a live animal
  tough meat   a fair decision   live music

2 a clear sky   4 a hard mattress   6 a light colour
  a clear conscience   a hard exam   a light sleeper

5 Match the words and their meanings.

1 **ab**used	not ever used
2 **dis**used	not used any more
3 **un**used	used cruelly or badly
4 **mis**used	used too much
5 **over**used	not used enough
6 **under**used	used in the wrong way

▶▶ **SONG** *I never loved you anyway* Teacher's Book *p145*

EVERYDAY ENGLISH
Being polite

1 What 'white lies' might you tell in these situations? Roleplay them with a partner.

> 1 You're having a meal with your host family. You've just forced yourself to eat something you don't like, when your host says, 'You must have some more!' What do you say?
>
> 2 A friend has just had a baby who you think looks like any other newborn baby. 'Isn't he gorgeous?' she coos. What do you say?
>
> 3 Your aunt invites you to go on holiday with her for two weeks. You love her, but know it would be a disaster and it would be no holiday for you. What do you say?

2 **T 4.9** Listen to the pairs of lines and conversations. After each one say which is more polite. In what ways? Look at the tapescript on p75 and practise the polite conversations with a partner.

3 Make these requests and offers more polite. Use the expressions below.

1 Give me a lift.
2 Help me find my glasses!
3 Come for a meal tomorrow evening!
4 Lend me your dictionary.
5 Look after my dog while I'm on holiday.
6 Where's the toilet?
7 Can I help you with this exercise?
8 Stop whistling!

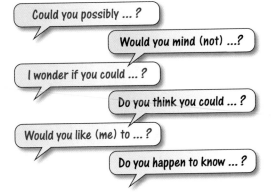

> Could you possibly ... ?
> Would you mind (not) ...?
> I wonder if you could ... ?
> Do you think you could ... ?
> Would you like (me) to ... ?
> Do you happen to know ... ?

Music of English 🎵🎵

To sound polite, start quite high and go even higher on the main stressed word. Your voice should then fall and rise at the end of the sentence.

Could you possibly close the window, please?

T 4.10 Listen and repeat. If you use flat intonation, it sounds very aggressive in English!

---

4 Work with a partner. Take turns to make the requests and offers in exercise 3 and refuse them politely, using one of these expressions.

I'd love to, but ...
I'm terribly sorry ...
I'm afraid I ...
That's really kind of you, but ...
Believe me, I would if I could, but ...

T 4.11 Listen and compare your answers.

Roleplay

5 Anna and Ben have invited their friends Kim and Henry to their house for dinner. Look at the conversation on p92. Work in groups of four to complete the conversation and then practise it, using the main stress shading to help you.

B Kim! Hello! Great to see you. Come on in. Let me take your coat.

Kim Thanks very much. Oh, these are for you.

T 4.12 Listen and compare.

5 An eye to the future

Future forms · Hot verbs – *take, put* · Telephoning

TEST YOUR GRAMMAR

1 Which future form expresses …?

| an intention | a prediction | a future fact based on a timetable | an arrangement between people | a spontaneous decision | a suggestion |

1 Tomorrow's weather will be warm and sunny.
2 The train to Dover leaves at ten past ten.
3 I'm going to be a racing driver when I grow up.

4 We're seeing Sue for lunch on Thursday.
5 Shall we have a break now?
6 I'll make some coffee.

2 Name the different future forms.

HOW DO YOU SEE YOUR FUTURE?
Future forms

1 **T 5.1** Look at the pictures and listen to these people talking about the future. Who says what? Put a number 1–6 next to the names.

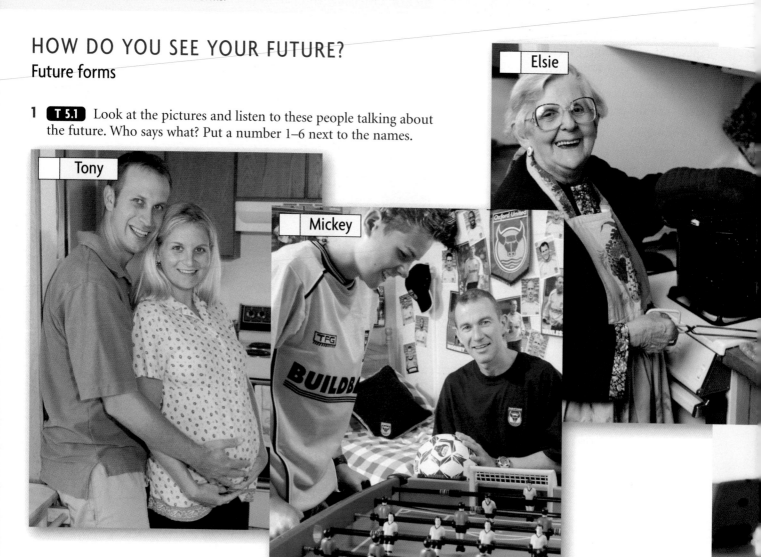

Elsie

Tony

Mickey

Katrina

Janine

Gavin

2 Answer the questions.

1 What is Katrina going to study?
   How long does her course last?
2 What is Mickey doing tomorrow?
   What time does the match start?
3 Why are Tony and Marie excited?
4 What's Elsie doing tomorrow?
   What will they do together?
5 Why is Janine packing?
   How's she getting to the airport?
6 What are Gavin's ambitions?

T 5.2 Listen and check.

3 Here are the answers to some questions.
Write the questions.

1 Bristol University. (*Which ...?*)
2 His son and some friends.
   Oxford United and Bristol Rovers.
3 Jamie or Hatty.
4 A sponge cake with jam in it.
5 It leaves at 10.30.
6 Twice what he's earning now.

T 5.3 Listen and check.

LANGUAGE FOCUS

1 Do these sentences refer to the present
or the future?

Marie's having a baby soon ...
At the moment I'm packing ...

I work in the City.
The plane leaves at 10.30.

2 What's the difference between these
sentences?

*What **do** you **do** in the evenings?*
*What **are** you **doing** this evening?*

*Get in the car. I'**ll give** you a lift.*
*I'**m going to give** Dave a lift to the
   airport tomorrow.*

*We'**ll have** supper at 8.00.*
*We'**ll be having** supper at 8.00.*

*I'**ll write** the report tonight.*
*I'**ll have** written the report by tonight.*

▶▶ **Grammar Reference pp84–85**

PRACTICE

Discussing grammar

1 Choose the correct form in the pairs of sentences.

1 'll see / 'm going to see

I'm very excited. I _____ all my family this weekend.

I don't know if I have time to come this evening. I _____ .

2 are you going to do / will you do

So you're off to the States for a year! What _____ there?

I'm sure you will pass your exams, but what _____ if you don't?

3 'll come / 'm coming

I _____ with you if you like.

I _____ with you whether you like it or not.

4 are you doing / are you going to do

Your school report is terrible. What _____ about it?

What _____ this evening?

5 'm giving / 'm going to give

I've had enough of her lazy attitude. I _____ her a good talking to.

I _____ a presentation at 3.00 this afternoon. I'm scared stiff.

6 leaves / is leaving

John! Peter _____ now. Come and say goodbye.

The coach _____ at 8.00, so don't be late.

7 'll see / 'll be seeing

I _____ you outside the cinema at 8.00.

I _____ Peter this afternoon, so I'll tell him your news.

8 'll see / 'll have seen

You _____ enough of me by the end of this holiday.

I'm going to make a success of my life. You _____ .

T 5.4 Listen and check.

2 Put the verb in brackets in the correct tense. Use Present Simple, Present Perfect, *will* or the Future Continuous.

'This is your captain speaking...'

Good morning, ladies and gentlemen. Welcome on board this British Airways flight to Rome. In a very short time we (1)_____ (take) off. When we (2)_____ (reach) our cruising speed of 550 miles per hour, we (3)_____ (fly) at 35,000 feet. Our flight time today is two and a half hours, so we (4)_____ (be) in Rome in time for lunch!

The cabin crew (5)_____ (serve) refreshments during the flight. If you (6)_____ (need) any assistance, just press the button and a flight attendant (7)_____ (come) to help you.

[*Near the end of the flight*]
In a few moments' time, the crew (8)_____ (come) round with duty-free goods. We (9)_____ also _____ (give out) landing cards. When you (10) _____ (fill) them in, place them in your passport. They (11)_____ (collect) as you (12)_____ (go) through passport control.

In twenty minutes' time we (13)_____ (land) at Leonardo da Vinci airport. Please put your seats in the upright position. You are requested to remain seated until the plane (14) _____ (come) to a complete standstill.

We hope you (15)_____ (fly) again soon with British Airways.

T 5.5 Listen and check.

3 Complete the sentences with the correct form of the verb. Use *will*, the Future Continuous, or the Future Perfect.

go

1 I can book the tickets. I _____ past the theatre on my way home.
2 I'll say goodbye now. You _____ by the time I get back.
3 He _____ mad when I tell him I've crashed his car.

make

4 'Tea?' 'It's OK. I _____ it.'
5 Dave is so ambitious. I bet he _____ a fortune by the time he's thirty.
6 You'll know where the party is. We _____ so much noise!

read

7 I'll lend you this book next time I see you. I _____ it by then.
8 We're studying Shakespeare next term so I _____ his plays over the summer.
9 I've just got an email from Megan. I _____ it to you.

Talking about you

4 Complete the questions with the most natural future form. Sometimes there are several possibilities.

1 Where _____ (you go) on holiday this year?
2 How _____ (you get) there?
3 How long _____ (you be) away for?
4 Which hotel _____ (you stay) in?
5 What time _____ (your flight arrive)?
6 What _____ (you do) while you're on holiday?

In pairs, ask and answer the questions about your next holiday. If you haven't got a holiday planned, make one up!

I hope so/I don't think so

5 **T 5.6** Listen to the conversations and complete them.

1 'Do you think you'll ever be rich?'
  'I _____ so.'
  'I _____ one day.'
  'It's possible, but I _____ it.'
  'I'm sure I _____.'
  'I'm sure I _____.'

2 'Are you going out tonight?'
  'Yes, I am.'
  'I think _____, but I'm not sure.'
  'I _____ be.'

3 'Do you think the world's climate will change dramatically in the next fifty years?'
  'I _____ so.'
  'I hope _____.'
  'Who _____? Maybe.'

6 Ask and answer similar yes/no questions about future possibilities in your life.

1 be famous
  go to Florida
  marry a millionaire
  speak perfect English
  have grandchildren

2 go to the cinema soon
  meet friends this weekend
  eat out in the next few days

3 we discover life on another planet
  people live for 150 years
  find a cure for cancer

TRAIN DE NOËL POUR
CHAMONIX
3 JOURS AUX SPORTS D'HIVER

INDIA

COTE D'AZUR
TOUTE L'ANNÉE

IMPERIAL
AIRWAYS

47

1 How do people of different ages see each other?

In your country, what do ...

- old people think of young people?
- young people think of old people?
- parents think of teenagers?
- teenagers think of their parents?
- people think of students?

2 A group of 18–24 year-olds were canvassed for their opinions. Here is a list of ten social issues they said they cared about. What do you think their order of importance was?

- [ ] Improving public transport
- [ ] Raising standards in schools
- [ ] Reducing crime levels
- [ ] Improving the National Health Service
- [ ] Increasing the amount of aid we give to developing countries
- [ ] Ending the arms trade
- [ ] Ending globalization
- [ ] Addressing the causes of global warming
- [ ] Redistributing wealth from the richest to the poorest
- [ ] Ensuring equal rights for everyone, regardless of gender, sexual orientation, colour, or religion

Look at the correct order on p93.
Would your personal order be different?

3 Look at the heading and sub-heading of the newspaper article. What are the contrasting ideas in the sub-heading? What is the complaint of these young people?

4 Read the article. What are some of the surprise findings of the poll? What are some of the frustrations of these young adults? How do they spend their leisure time?

WE WORK, WE VOTE, WE CARE' ...

Selfish, work-shy, and uninterested in how their country and the world are governed – that is the popular view of our young adults. In fact, a new survey shows they are conscientious, idealistic, and care deeply about important issues, but feel they have no voice. Damian Whitworth and Carol Midgley report.

THIS is a story about people who believe that no one is listening.

They are concerned citizens, keenly aware that it is their civic duty to vote in the next general election, despite their disillusionment with politics and political leaders.

They worry about the future of the National Health Service, crime and schools, not trendy 'youth' issues such as legalizing soft drugs. They like to save their money, but are shouldering heavy debts. They have clear career plans.

This is the surprising picture of today's 18 to 24-year-olds. It is confirmed in numerous interviews, and in a huge number of emails from readers in response to our request to tell us how the world looks from early adulthood.

Perhaps the most intriguing findings relate to politics, where the message is that young people are alienated from politicians, but not from the issues. Nine out of ten say 'We all have a responsibility to vote'.

Two thirds say 'the main parties are so much alike that it doesn't make much difference who is in power'. 71 per cent say that 'politics matters, but political parties have nothing to say on the really important issues'.

> **Nine out of ten say 'We all have a responsibility to vote'.**

Almost half think that their parents' generation has no idea what it is like to be a young adult today. Two thirds think their grandparents are unaware of what it is to be young in the 21st century.

How do these people spend their time? Buying clothes is top, followed by purchasing and listening to CDs, both of which are well ahead of going to clubs, bars, and pubs. Next is eating out, and then drinking alcohol. Travel, going to the cinema or theatre, and reading books all came above sporting events and gigs and concerts, which came bottom of the list.

BUT NOBODY LISTENS TO US

www.stopwar.org.uk

5 Read the case studies on p50. Which person might have said ...?

1 I'm going to work and work.
2 I'm thinking of being self-employed.
3 This time next year I'll be living abroad.
4 I hope I'll have paid off my debts by the time I'm 31.
5 I certainly won't be working here forever.
6 I'll never be able to buy my own place.
7 I'm seeing my bank manager this afternoon to talk about getting a mortgage.

6 What is Amber's worry? Ellie's? Peter's?
What is Bob's intention? Kylie's? Joe's? Alex's?

What do you think?

- Are the frustrations and aspirations mentioned in the text similar to those of young people in your country?
- What are your aspirations for the future?

Language work

Complete the chart of adjectives and nouns. Mark the stress. The missing words are all in the article on p48.

Adjective	Noun
'popular	popu'larity
	awareness
disillusioned	
political	(x2)
criminal	
	intrigue
	alienation
responsible	
different	
powerful	

SPOKEN ENGLISH *thing*

Look at the examples of the word *thing* in the text.

> The thing is, a lot of social problems never seem to get dealt with properly.
> Politics just isn't my kind of thing.

The word *thing* is used a lot in English! In pairs, ask and answer the questions about you.

- How are things with you at the moment?
- What's the thing you like most about your best friend?
- Generally speaking, do you try to do the right thing?
- Do you like doing your own thing?
- Is horse racing your kind of thing?
- Do you ever say the wrong thing in company?
- Do you have a thing about people wearing fur?
- If your friend keeps you waiting, do you make a big thing of it?

Listen to us!

We carried out our own survey of the views of young people:

AMBER HONESS, 21
Student at Bristol University

This is my final year at university. I've been doing business studies for three years. Some of my friends will be going into finance companies; others don't really know what they'll be doing this time next year. But I know what I want to do – open a clothes shop with a friend of mine. We've got some great ideas.

My parents helped me a lot with money, but I still have debts of about £10,000. Terrifying, isn't it? It'll probably take me ten years to pay it off.

ELLIE GREEN, 24
Corporate lawyer

Young people are interested in politics, but it's very frustrating because you don't feel you can really make a difference.

The thing is, a lot of social problems never seem to get dealt with properly. We still have homeless people, the NHS doesn't seem to work no matter how much money is thrown at it, and more and more old people don't have adequate pensions.

I'm buying a house with my boyfriend soon, because I want to get on the property ladder before it's too late. I only hope I manage to keep my job. If that goes, I've had it. So I'm not very optimistic about the future.

PETER JAMIESON, 24
Trainee manager from Belfast

When my parents were young, they didn't have to worry about finding a secure job with prospects of promotion. They seemed to be a lot more relaxed about the future. These days we're put under pressure to get ahead in the rat race. No wonder so many young people take drugs.

One thing that really worries me is the cost of housing. I share a house with four other blokes, and I'll probably be living here for ever. There's no way I'll ever be able to afford a house of my own.

> **"I don't think any of them know what it's like to be our age nowadays."**

BOB WEST, 25
Plumber, London

I've never yet voted for the winning side in an election. Whoever I vote for, loses. So I guess I'm doing something wrong, somewhere. I still think it's important to vote, though. Let's face it, people would soon kick up a fuss if they weren't allowed to.

I'm saving money, and as soon as my application has been processed, I'm going to leave the country and live in Canada. Now there's a country that encourages young people and enterprise!

KYLIE WILLIAMSON, 24
Loans department in a bank

Politics just isn't my kind of thing. Dry, dull people, who bleat on about the same old things. I don't think any of them know what it's like to be our age nowadays.

A decent income is what matters to me, and as soon as I can, I'm going to start my own business.

JOE CASWELL, 20
Engineering student at Edinburgh

I know that if I don't graduate, I'll end up working in a dead-end job, just like my dad. So I know what I'm going to do – work my backside off to prove to my mum and dad that I can make it.

ALEX WILLIAMS, 24
Marketing account manager

There's no such thing as a job for life these days. Employers can make you redundant as soon as there's a downturn, so people don't feel the same loyalty. A lot of my friends are changing jobs to boost their career prospects. I expect I'll have several jobs before I'm 30, and I hope that in my working life I'll have several careers. I don't want to do the same thing for ever. I'm going for an interview next week. More money, more responsibility. 'Don't put off till tomorrow what you can do today' is my motto.

VOCABULARY
Hot verbs – *take, put*

1 There are many expressions with *take* and *put*. Look at these examples from the text on p50.

> It'll probably **take me ten years** to pay (the debt) off.
> These days we're **put under pressure** to get ahead in the rat race.
> No wonder so many young people **take drugs**.
> Don't **put off** till tomorrow what you can do today.

2 Put the words in the right box.

> offence   a stop to sth   place   your arm round sb   (no) notice   part
> sb in charge of sth   sb/sth for granted   my advice   a plan into practice
> a risk   your work first   responsibility for sth   pressure on sb   ages

TAKE	PUT

3 Complete the sentences with expressions from exercise 2 in the correct form.

1 The wedding _____ _____ in an old country church. It was lovely, but it was miles away. It _____ _____ to get there.

2 My son's buying cigarettes, but I'll soon _____ _____ _____ to that. I won't give him any more pocket money.

3 Please don't _____ _____ but I don't think your work has been up to your usual standard recently.

4 I told you that boy was no good for you. You should have _____ _____ _____ and had nothing to do with him.

5 The older you get, the more you have to learn to _____ _____ for your own life.

6 My boss is _____ _____ on me to resign, but I won't go.

7 I tried to get the teacher's attention but she _____ _____ _____ of me at all.

8 Children never say 'Thank you' or 'How are you?' to their parents. They just _____ them _____ _____.

T 5.7 Listen and check.

4 Match a line in **A** with a line in **B**. Underline the expressions with *take* or *put*.

A	B
1 Take your time.	Put it in your diary.
2 The party's on the 21st.	What would you do?
3 Their relationship will never last.	Calm down. There's no need to panic.
4 'I told her a joke about the French, and it turned out she *was* French.'	There's no need to hurry.
5 Take it easy.	No one's out to get you.
6 Put yourself in my shoes.	Take my word for it. I know these things.
7 You always take things too personally.	'Whoops! You really put your foot in it, didn't you?'

Phrasal verbs

5 Use a dictionary. Complete the sentences with a phrasal verb with *take*.

> take sth back   take sth in
> take off   take sb on

1 The shop _____ _____ a lot of extra staff every Christmas.

2 The lecture was too complicated, and the students couldn't _____ it all _____.

3 My business really _____ _____ after I picked up six new clients.

4 You called me a liar, but I'm not. _____ that _____ and say sorry!

T 5.8 Listen and check.

6 Complete the sentences with these phrasal verbs with *put*.

> put sth out   put sb off
> put sth away   put sth on

1 _____ some music _____! Whatever you want.

2 That article about factory farming has really _____ me _____ eating chicken.

3 Could you _____ _____ your clothes, please. Your room's a total mess.

4 _____ your cigarette _____! You can't smoke in here.

T 5.9 Listen and check.

'Well, I wouldn't eat it, but don't let that put you off.'

LISTENING AND SPEAKING
The reunion

1 Three friends, Alan, Sarah, and James, were all at university together in Durham, a town in the north of England. Now, ten years later, they are planning a reunion. Divide into two groups.

Group A
T 5.10 Listen to Alan phoning Sarah.

Group B
T 5.11 Listen to Sarah phoning James.

Listen and complete as much as possible of the chart. The following names are mentioned.

Claypath	the Lotus Garden	the Midlands
The County	The Three Tuns	Leeds
the Kwai Lam	Saddler Street	Sunderland

2 Check your answers with people in your group.

	Alan	Sarah	James
Travelling from?			
How?			
Leaving at what time?			
Arriving in Durham at?			
Staying where?			
Going to which restaurant?			
Where is it?			
Where are they going to meet?			
What time?			

3 Find a partner from the other group. Swap information to complete the chart.

4 What might go wrong with their arrangements? Or will everything work out all right? Who's meeting who where?

▶▶ **WRITING** Emailing friends *p67*

Alan   Sarah   James

EVERYDAY ENGLISH

Beginning a telephone conversation

1 **T 5.12** Listen to the beginning of three phone calls. What's the difference between them?

- When and why do we make small talk? Who with? What about?
- Why do organizations have recorded menus?
- Why do people find them frustrating?

2 Here is the beginning of a telephone conversation between two people who *don't* know each other. Put it in the right order.

- ☐ **1** Hello. TVS Computers. Samantha speaking. How can I help you?
- ☐ (*pause*) OK. It's ringing for you now.
- ☐ Yes, please.
- ☐ (*ring ring*) Hello. Customer services.
- ☐ Good morning. Could I speak to your customer services department, please?
- ☐ (*pause*) I'm afraid the line's busy at the moment. Will you hold?
- ☐ Certainly. Who's calling?
- ☐ Thank you.
- ☐ This is Keith Jones.
- ☐ **10** Hello, I was wondering if you could help me ...

T 5.13 Listen and check your answers.

Ending a telephone conversation

3 Here is the end of a telephone conversation between two work colleagues, Andy and Barry. Put it in the right order.

- ☐ **1** **A** So, Barry. It was good to talk to you. Thanks very much for phoning.
- ☐ **A** I certainly will. And you'll send me a copy of the report?
- ☐ **A** That's great, Barry. Have a good weekend!
- ☐ **B** My pleasure. By the way, how's your golf these days? Still playing?
- ☐ **B** Same to you, too! Bye, Andy.
- ☐ **B** OK. Don't want to keep you. So, you'll give me a ring when you're back, right?
- ☐ **A** No, not much. I just don't seem to find the time these days. Anyway, Barry ...
- ☐ **B** It'll be in the post tonight.
- ☐ **A** It's true. Right, Barry. I must fly. I'm late for a meeting.
- ☐ **B** What a shame! You used to enjoy it so much.
- ☐ **11** **A** Bye, Barry.

T 5.14 Listen and check your answers.

4 Discuss the questions.
- Who's trying to end the conversation?
- Who wants to chat?
- How does Andy try to signal that he wants to end the conversation?
- How do they confirm their arrangements?

5 Your teacher will give you a list of expressions and a role card for a phone conversation. Work in pairs. Decide if you think small talk is necessary, and if so, what you can talk about. Sit back to back and have the conversation.

6 Making it big

Expressions of quantity · **'export and ex'port** · **Business expressions and numbers**

TEST YOUR GRAMMAR

1 <u>Underline</u> the words that can complete the expressions of quantity.

a few ... cars/traffic/hold-ups/pollution
not many ... crimes/criminals/violence/accidents
several ... times/letters/paper/rooms

very little ... time/room/hope/spaces
not much ... jobs/unemployment/work/experience
a bit of ... luck/opportunity/fun/help

a lot of ... enthusiasm/energy/people/ingredients
enough ... chairs/food/herbs/cutlery
plenty of ... fresh air/fluids/sleep/walks
hardly any ... money/experience/clothes/friends

2 What do you notice about the three groups of quantifiers?

THE NAKED CHEF
Expressions of quantity

1 Jamie Oliver is a famous British chef. Read the article. Why do you think he is called *the Naked Chef*?

2 Answer the questions.

1 How many TV series has he made?
2 How many books has he written?
3 How many live shows does he do a year?
4 How much did he earn cooking at his parents' pub?
5 How long did he spend in catering college?
6 How much time did he spend in France?
7 How many chefs did he work under in London?
8 How much experience did he have when he was first on TV?
9 How many fresh ingredients and herbs did he use?
10 How much interest in food programmes did his audience have previously?

Jamie Oliver

At only 28, JAMIE OLIVER is now an extremely successful and well-known chef, with his own acclaimed restaurant in the centre of London. He has made five TV series, written several books, and still does around twenty live shows a year. He doesn't have much free time any more. How did he make it big?

Well, his rise to fame and fortune came early and swiftly. By the age of eight he had already started cooking at his parents' pub. It was an easy way to earn a bit of pocket money! After two years in catering college, and some time spent in France, he started working in restaurants. He worked under three famous chefs in London before he was spotted by a TV producer at 21, and his life changed.

Even though he had very little experience, he had a great deal of enthusiasm for cooking, and was very natural in front of the camera. His first TV programme featured him zipping around London on his scooter buying ingredients and cooking for his friends, all to a rock and roll soundtrack. The recipes were bare and simple – they didn't involve complicated cooking techniques and used plenty of fresh ingredients and herbs. It attracted a completely new audience that previously had no interest in food programmes. Jamie Oliver became an overnight success.

So what's his recipe for success? 'A little bit of luck, a little bit of passion, and a little bit of knowledge!' he says.

3 **T 6.1** Listen to a similar text about Jamie Oliver. Write down the differences you hear.

4 Close your books. What can you remember about Jamie Oliver?

PRACTICE

Countable or uncountable?

1 With a partner, ask and answer questions.

How much ...?   **How many ...?**

1 money/in your pocket
2 cups of coffee/day
3 times/been on a plane
4 time/spend watching TV
5 sugar/in your coffee
6 pairs of jeans
7 books/read in one year
8 homework/a night
9 English teachers/had
10 films/a month

T 6.2 Listen and compare your answers.

2 Some nouns can be both countable (**C**) or uncountable (**U**).

Chocolate is fattening. **U**
Have a chocolate. **C**

I do a lot of business in Russia. **U**
We opened a business together. **C**

Complete the sentences with *a* or nothing.

1 I'd like ___ single room for the night.
   Is there ___ room for me to sit down?

2 You mustn't let children play with ___ fire.
   Can we light ___ fire? It's getting cold.

3 Scotland is a land of ___ great beauty.
   You should see my new car. It's ___ beauty.

4 There was ___ youth standing in front of me.
   ___ youth is wasted on the young.

3 Find word pairs linked according to meaning. Which are normally count nouns, and which uncount? Write them in the correct column.

~~dollar~~   lorry   suitcase   job   furniture   advice   apple
trouble   fact   ~~money~~   suggestion   fruit   journey   chair
problem   work   traffic   information   luggage   travel

Count nouns	Uncount nouns
dollar	money

With a partner, choose a pair of words. Write two sentences to illustrate their use. Use the count nouns in the plural.

We need some new furniture.   **We need four more chairs.**

Expressing quantity

4 Rephrase the sentences. Use the prompts.

She earns five euros an hour.

  much / very little / hardly any

  She doesn't earn much money.
  She earns very little money.
  She earns hardly any money.

1 She's got two friends.

  many / very few / hardly any

2 There are six eggs in the fridge.

  some / a few / enough

3 There are two eggs in the fridge.

  many / only a couple of

4 There aren't any tomatoes.

  no / not a single / none

5 Did you spend many weeks in France?

  much / a lot of

6 I have five days' holiday a year.

  much / hardly any

7 I have put on 20 kilos!

  a huge amount of / far too much / loads of

8 Ninety per cent of my friends have a car.

  almost all / most / the majority

9 Ten percent of them smoke.

  very few / hardly any / not many

10 There isn't one of my friends who's married.

  none / not one

11 Ken works 100 per cent of the time.

  all / the whole

12 Yesterday I ate hardly anything at all.

  not much / very little / almost nothing

5 Choose the correct alternative.

1 I have *a few / few* cousins, but not many.

2 We have *very little / a little* money, I'm afraid.

3 I earn *less / fewer* money than I did in my old job!

4 *Less / fewer* people go to church these days.

5 *All people / Everyone* came to my party.

6 I was burgled last month. *All / Everything* was stolen.

7 *Everyone / All the people* was watching the Cup Final.

8 Last week the *all / whole* school had flu.

> ### SPOKEN ENGLISH Expressing quantity
>
> There are many ways of expressing quantity in spoken English.
> *She's got **loads of** clothes.*
>
> **T 6.3** Listen and fill the gaps with the expression of quantity you hear.
>
> _____ of time   _____ of food   _____ of things
> _____ of money   _____ of washing _____ of people
>
> What have your friends got a lot of?
> *Tania's got millions of boyfriends.*

A lifestyle survey

Conduct a survey of the habits of your class using the activities listed. When you are ready, give your feedback using expressions from the box.

- like shopping
- spend a lot of money on trainers
- watch *Friends*
- buy designer clothes
- like *The Simpsons*
- go to coffee shops
- go clubbing regularly
- do a lot of exercise

> all of us
> most of us
> a few of us
> hardly anybody
> quite a lot of us
> nobody
> (nearly) everybody
> none of us

Most of us like shopping.

WRITING Report writing – A consumer survey *p68*

LISTENING AND SPEAKING
Advertisements

1 What's your favourite advertisement at the moment? What's it for? Does it have a story?

2 Talk about an advertisement from a newspaper or magazine. What's it for? Why do you like it?

3 **T 6.4** Listen to six radio advertisements and answer the questions. Write a number 1–6.

Which advert ...

... is advertising a football match? ☐
... is selling a chocolate bar? ☐
... is selling soap powder? ☐
... is for a new car with free insurance? ☐
... is for car insurance for women? ☐
... is advertising a shop's opening hours? ☐

4 Complete the chart.

	Name of the product	Characters involved	Setting/ place
1			
2			
3			
4			
5			
6			

5 What is the selling point for each advert?

6 Answer the questions about each advert.

1 Describe Sarah's play shirt.
What's special about this washing powder?

2 What do the men think of the woman driver?
Why and how do they change their minds?

3 What has the daughter done that she's so proud of?
Why is her father so horrible to her?

4 How can the daughter afford a new car?
In what ways does she make fun of her father?

5 What does the man want to invite Sue to do?
In what ways does he say the wrong thing?

6 How does the vicar try to hurry up the wedding?
Why is he in a hurry?

Writing an advert

Devise a radio or television advert. Choose a product or service of your own, or one of the following.

a BMW sports car   Bonzo dog food
    Dazzle washing-up liquid
Blue Mountain coffee   a bank for students
    a restaurant in town
        a computer

STARBUCKS COFFEE

1 What do you know about these brands? What is their reputation? Are they popular among your friends and family? Who are their rivals?

2 Work in two groups.

Group A Read about Starbucks on this page.
Group B Read about Apple Macintosh on p59.

Read your article and answer the questions.

1 When and where did the company begin?
2 Who founded it?
3 Where did the name of the company come from?
4 Why did the product become a success?
5 Has the company's progress always been easy?
6 What makes the brand special?
7 What features of the product or company do people see as negative?
8 What are some examples of the company's products?

3 Find a partner from the other group. Compare and swap information.

4 Here are eight answers. Decide which four are about your article. Then write the questions.

- In Silicon Valley.
- Three or four.
- $5 billion.
- In 1997. (*When ... launched?*)
- Ten years. (*How long ... take ... ?*)
- Because he argued with his partner. (*Why ... resign?*)
- Because they can't compete. (*Why ... out of business?*)
- By selling some of their possessions. (*How ... ?*)

ANYONE FOR COFFEE? What about a Skinny Latte, or perhaps an Almond Truffle Mocha, or even a Raspberry Mocha Chip Frappuccino? These are just a few of the many speciality coffees on offer at Starbucks, the world's leading coffee roaster and retailer.

Starbucks serves over 25 million customers a week in 7,500 stores around the world. And this figure is increasing rapidly, with three or four new stores being opened every single day! So how did a company currently worth $5 billion get started?

Starbucks Coffee, Tea and Spice, as it was originally known, roasted its first coffee beans in 1971. This tiny coffee house in Seattle, named after a character in the novel *Moby Dick*, was the vision of three men – Baldwin, Siegel, and Bowker – who cared passionately about fine coffee and tea. Their determination to provide the best quality coffee helped their business to succeed, and a decade later, their fourth store in Seattle opened.

Meanwhile, in New York, Howard Schultz, a businessman specializing in kitchen equipment, noticed that a small company in Seattle was ordering a large number of a special type of coffeemaker. Out of curiosity, he made the cross-country trip to Seattle to find out more. Immediately he saw the Starbucks store, he knew that he wanted to be part of it. The three founder members weren't initially very keen, but a persistent Schultz was eventually hired to be head of Starbucks marketing in 1982. He modelled the Starbucks stores on Italian espresso bars, and made them comfortable places to relax. Within the next ten years, Schultz had already opened 150 new stores and had bought the company! There are now stores all over Europe, Asia, and the Middle East. Today Starbucks is one of the world's most recognized brands.

"3 or 4 new stores open every day."

But global success comes at a price. Although Starbucks has a company policy of fair trade and employee welfare, it has been the recent target of anti-globalization protests. Many people feel that big corporations, even responsible ones, are never a good thing, as small, independent companies can't compete and go out of business. However, Starbucks' continued success in the face of opposition shows that its blend of commercialism and comfy sofas is still proving an irresistible recipe for world domination.

Apple Macintosh

ARE YOU A MAC USER? For many, home computers have become synonymous with Windows and Bill Gates, but there has always been a loyal band of Apple Macintosh users, whose devotion to the Apple brand and its co-founder Steven Jobs is almost religious.

Steven Jobs and Steven Wozniak dropped out of college and got jobs in Silicon Valley, where they founded the Apple Computer company in 1976, the name based on Jobs' favourite fruit. They designed the Apple I computer in Jobs' bedroom, having raised the capital by selling their most valued possessions – an old Volkswagen bus and a scientific calculator. The later model, the Apple Macintosh, introduced the public to point and click graphics. It was the first home computer to be truly user-friendly, or as the first advertising campaign put it, 'the computer for the rest of us'.

When IBM released its first PC in 1981, Jobs realized that Apple would have to become a more grown-up company in order to compete effectively. He brought in John Sculley, the president of Pepsi-Cola, to do the job, asking him 'Do you want to just sell sugared water for the rest of your life, or do you want to change the world?' Sculley and Jobs began to argue bitterly, however, and after a power struggle, Jobs was reluctantly forced to resign.

"The computer for the rest of us."

By 1996 Apple was in trouble, due to the dominance of Windows software and the increasing number of PC clones which could use it. Jobs, having had great success with his animation studio Pixar, was brought back to the ailing firm for an annual salary of $1, and the company gradually returned to profitability.

Apple's computers cost more than most PCs, and have a more limited range of software available for them, but their great appeal has been the attention to design, making Apple the cool computer company. The launch of the stunning multi-coloured iMac in 1997, followed by the sleek new iMac in 2002, marked the end of the computer as an ugly, utilitarian machine, and brought the home computer out of the study and into the lounge. As Steve Jobs put it, 'Other companies don't care about design. We think it's vitally important.'

Apple's fortunes were transformed again with the development of the iPod in 2003, which soon became a must-have gadget and brought about a boom in Internet music sales. And of course, it was beautifully stylish.

Vocabulary work

Find adverbs ending in *-ly* in the texts that have these meanings.

Starbucks

a	at great speed
b	at the present time
c	in the beginning, before a change
d	with strong feeling and enthusiasm
e	at the beginning
f	after a long time, especially after a delay

Apple Macintosh

a	really/genuinely
b	in a way that produces a successful result
c	in a way that shows feelings of sadness or anger
d	in a way that shows hesitation because you don't want to do sth
e	slowly over a long period of time
f	in a very important way

What do you think?

1 What arguments do the anti-globalization protesters make against Starbucks and other multinational corporations? Do you agree?

2 Do you have a computer? What sort? What are your favourite websites?

VOCABULARY AND PRONUNCIATION
export: /'ekspɔːt/ or /ɪk'spɔːt/?

1 [T 6.5] Listen and repeat these words, first as nouns and then as verbs. How does the word stress change?

a export	c decrease	e progress	g refund	i permit	k insult
b import	d increase	f record	h produce	j transport	l protest

2 With a partner practise the words. Give instructions like this.

> *c as a noun!*   'decrease

> *g as a verb!*   re'fund

3 Complete the sentences with one of the words in its correct form. Read the sentences aloud.

1 Scotland _____ a lot of its food from other countries. Its _____ include oil, beef, and whisky.
2 I'm very pleased with my English. I'm making a lot of _____.
3 Ministers are worried. There has been an _____ in the number of unemployed.
4 But the number of crimes has _____, so that's good news.
5 How dare you call me a liar and a cheat! What an _____!
6 There was a demonstration yesterday. People were _____ about blood sports.
7 He ran 100m in 9.75 seconds and broke the world _____.
8 Don't touch the DVD player! I'm _____ a film.
9 Britain _____ about 50% of its own oil.

[T 6.6] Listen and check.

refuse: /'refjuːs/ or /rɪ'fjuːz/?

1 [T 6.7] These words have different meanings according to the stress. Check the meaning, part of speech, and the pronunciation in your dictionary. Listen and repeat.

a refuse	c minute	e content	g invalid
b present	d desert	f object	h contract

2 Practise saying the words in exercise 1 with a partner.

> *g as an adjective!*   in'valid

3 Answer the questions using the words in exercise 1.

1 What's another name for a dustman?
2 What's a UFO?
3 What's the Sahara?
4 What do you get lots of on your birthday?
5 What are pages 2 to 5 of this book?
6 What's another way of saying ...?
 • happy   • very small
 • a written agreement   • to say you won't do something
 • incorrect (PIN number)

[T 6.8] Listen and check.

SPEAKING
A business maze

Work in small groups.

> You have reached one of life's crossroads! You've been made redundant, and some big decisions about your future have to be made.

Discuss the problem on the card until you all agree on what to do next.

1

You were working as a chef in a large restaurant. You have been made redundant, as the restaurant is being converted into a cinema. You have received £15,000 redundancy money. You have a family to support, and cannot survive for long without an income. You want to start a restaurant in your local town, as you believe there is a need for one. It is going to require more than your £15,000, so what are you going to do?

Approach the bank for the extra funding to get your plans underway?
GO TO 8

Go into business with a partner. A friend of yours was also made redundant and received the same amount of money. Why not do it together?
GO TO 22

Your teacher will give you your next card with more information and more decisions. Keep discussing until you get out of the maze. You might succeed, or you might fail!

What do you think?

• Appoint a spokesperson from each group.

Tell the rest of the class about the decisions that your group took.

In retrospect, did you make any wrong decisions?

• Why are activities such as these used for management training exercises?

EVERYDAY ENGLISH
Business expressions and numbers

1 This exercise practises fixed expressions in a work context. Match a line in **A** with a reply in **B**.

> We need to get together sometime. When would suit you best?

> Monday and Tuesday are out for me, but Wednesday would be fine. Let's say 9.30.

A	B
1 Mike! Long time no see! How are things?	a Sorry, I didn't quite get that last bit. What was it again?
2 I'm afraid something's come up, and I can't make our meeting on the 6th.	b Sure. I'll email them to you as an attachment.
3 What are your travel arrangements?	c Hey! Mind your own business! You wouldn't tell anyone yours!
4 Could you confirm the details in writing?	d There's no point. I'm not qualified for it. I wouldn't stand a chance.
5 They want a deposit of 2½ percent, which is £7,500, and we ... the two ... thousand ... ge... t...	e I'm getting flight BA 2762, at 18.45.
6 I'll give you £5,250 for your car. That's my final offer.	f Good, thanks, Jeff. Business is booming. What about yourself?
7 I don't know their number offhand. Bear with me while I look it up.	g Great! It's a deal. It's yours.
8 OK. Here's their number. Are you ready? It's 0800 205080.	h Never mind. Let's go for the following week. Is Wednesday the 13th good for you?
9 So what's your salary, Dave? 35K? 40K?	i No worries. I'll hold.
10 Have you applied for that job?	j I'll read that back to you. Oh eight double oh, two oh five, oh eight oh.

T 6.9 Listen and check.

2 Work with a partner. Cover the lines in **B**. Try to remember the conversations. Then cover the lines in **A** and do the same.

> ### Music of English 🎶
> Use the stress shading to help you get the rhythm of each sentence right.

'No. Thursday's out. How about never – is never good for you?'

3 Practise the numbers in the conversations. How is the phone number said in two different ways?

4 Practise saying these numbers.

375   1,250   13,962   23,806   150,000   5,378,212
½   ¾   ⅓   ¼   ⅔

4.3   7.08   10.5   3.142   0.05

17 Sept   Feb 3   22 Nov   Aug 14

19th century   21st century   1960s

2007   1980   1786   1902

12.00 p.m.   12.00 a.m.   14.05   22.30

07775 360722   0800 664733   0990 21 22 23

(football) 2 – 0   (tennis) 30 – 0

T 6.10 Listen and check.

5 Write down some numbers. Dictate them to your partner. Ask your partner to read them back to you.

Writing

1 What is a CV? What is the aim of one? Have you ever written one? What information did/would you include?

2 What is the purpose of a covering letter?

3 Write the headings from **A** in the correct spaces in the CV in **B**.

A

Profile	Additional information
Education	~~Name~~
References	Work experience
Personal details	Interests

4 Answer the questions.

1 Where did Kate go to school?
2 What did she study at university?
3 Who is Prof Jane Curtis?
4 Does she have a lot of work experience?

5 How is a CV different in your country?

B

Name _____

Kate Henderson

DOB 17/04/83

Address 31 Rendlesham Way
Watford
Herts
WD3 5GT

Phone 01923 984663
Mobile 07764 733689
Email katehenderson@hotshot.com

_____
A highly-motivated, well-travelled, and enthusiastic graduate, with practical experience of working with children of all ages.

_____
Watford Grammar School
8 GCSEs
3 A-levels
Bristol University
BA (Hons) Psychology and Education

_____
June 2000
Life guard and supervisor at KLC Leisure Centre
July 2001
Athletics coach at training centre
June 2003
Teaching assistant at secondary school

_____
Dance, athletics, volleyball, travel, cinema

_____
One of my main interests is dance, which I have done since I was three, passing many exams, and performing in annual dance festivals. I have organized sports events and training sessions for dance, athletics, and trampoline. I have travelled widely throughout the world, in Europe, the Far East, and the USA.

_____
Prof Jane Curtis
Dept of Education
Bristol University
BS5 7LA

Mike Benson
Head Teacher
Bailey School
Watford, Herts
WD3 8JG

6 This is the job that Kate is applying for. Is she well qualified for it?

> **ACTIVITY HOLIDAY ORGANIZER IN THE CANARY ISLANDS**
>
> *Are you …*
> - aged between 18–30?
> - energetic?
> - good at organizing people?
>
> *Do you …*
> - like kids?
> - like sport?
>
> **Then come and join us as a leader for an Easter holiday of fun, looking after groups of kids at sports camp!**
>
> **Send your CV to** Mark Sullivan at 106 Piccadilly, Bristol BS8 7TQ

7 Read Kate's covering letter. Which parts sound too informal? Replace them with words on the right.

31 Rendlesham Way
Watford
Herts
WD3 5GT

01923 984663

Mark Sullivan
106 Piccadilly
Bristol
BS8 7TQ

17 March 2004

Dear Mark

I am applying for the post of camp leader, which I saw advertised somewhere recently. Here's my CV.

I reckon I have just about everything needed for this job. I have worked loads with kids, doing all kinds of stuff. They generally do what I tell them, and we manage to have a great time together. Having studied psychology and education at university, I know quite a bit about the behaviour of kids.

I am really into sport, and have lots of experience of organizing training events. I am a very practical person, easy-going, and it's no problem for me to make friends. I've been all over the place, and enjoy meeting new people.

I can't wait to hear from you.

Best wishes

Kate Henderson

Kate Henderson

---

extensively with young adults

respect my leadership abilities

I find it easy

very interested in

have a certain understanding of

Please find enclosed

look forward to hearing

considerable

many of the relevant

qualifications

have travelled widely

Mr Sullivan

Yours sincerely

in the March edition of the magazine *Holiday Jobs for Graduates*

feel

organizing a variety of activities

establish a good working relationship

Is this how a formal letter is laid out in your country? What are the differences?

8 Write your CV and a covering letter for a job that you would really like to do and are well qualified for.

1 Teachers sometimes use these symbols when correcting written work.

Correct the mistakes in these sentences.

1 I ⋏ born in 1971 in <u>one</u>^{WW} small town in Mexico.

2 My father is ⋏ diplomat, so <u>my all life</u>^{WO} I <u>live</u>^T in <u>differents</u>^{Gr} countries.

3 After <s>the</s> school, I went <u>for four years</u>^{WO} <u>in</u>^{WW} a <u>busyness</u>^{Sp} college.

4 <u>I'm married</u>^T <u>since</u>^{Prep} five years. I <u>knew</u>^{WW} my wife while I was a student.

5 My town <u>isnt</u>^P as exciting <u>than</u>^{WW} London. ⋏ Is very <u>quite</u>^{Sp} <u>at</u>^{Prep} the evening.

6 I <u>learn</u>^T English for five years. I <u>start</u>^T when I <u>had</u>^{WW} eleven <s>years</s>.

7 My father <u>wants that I</u>^{Gr} work in a bank <u>becaus</u>^{Sp} ⋏ is a good <u>work</u>^{WW}.

8 I <u>do</u>^T <u>a</u>^{Gr} evening course in English. I enjoy <u>very much</u>^{WO} <u>to learn</u>^{Gr} languages.

WW	Wrong word
Sp	Spelling
T	Tense
Gr	Grammar
⋏	Word missing
P	Punctuation
Prep	Preposition
WO	Word order
/	This word isn't necessary

2 Read the letter. Answer the questions.
1 Where was the letter written?
2 Who is the guest? Who is the host?
3 Which city is described? What is it like?
4 What season is it?

3 Work with a partner. Find the mistakes and put the symbols on the letter. Then correct the mistakes. The first line has been done to help you.

4 Write a letter (about 250 words).

Either …
You are going to stay with a family in an English-speaking country.

Or …
An English-speaking guest is coming to stay with you.

Give some information about yourself – your family, interests, school, your town.

Check your work carefully for mistakes!

Avenida Campinas 361 ap. 45
01238 São Paulo Brasil

23 December

Dear James

Thank you ⋏^T your letter. I receive it ^{Gr} the last week. Sorry I no reply ⋏^T you before, but I've been very busy. It's Christmas soon, and everyone are very exciting!

In two weeks I am with you in England. I can no belief it! I looking forward meet you and your familly very much. I'm sure we will like us very well.

My city, São Paulo, is biggest and noisyest city in Brasil. Is not really for tourist. Is a centre commercial. Also it have very much pollution and traffic. But there is lot of things to do. I like very much listen music. There are bars who stay open all night!

My friend went in London last year, and he has seen a football match at Arsenal. He said me was wonderfull. I like to do that also.

My plane arrive to Heathrow at 6.30 am in 3 Janury. Is very kind you meet me so early morning.

I hope very much improve my english during I am with you!

See you soon and happy New Year!

Fernando

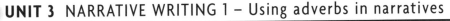

1 Have you ever been in a dangerous situation? Write some notes about when, where, who you were with, and what happened. Discuss your notes with a partner and compare the situations.

2 Put the adverbs or adverbial phrases in the correct place in these sentences. Sometimes more than one place is possible.

1 I used to go skiing.	*in winter, frequently*
2 I enjoyed going to Colorado.	*with my family, especially*
3 I had a bad accident.	*two years ago, then, really*
4 I skied into a tree.	*headfirst*
5 I broke my leg.	*in three places, unfortunately,*
6 I'd like to go skiing again.	*definitely, one day*
7 But I don't feel confident.	*yet, enough*
8 My family go skiing.	*however, still, every February*

Read the completed story aloud with your partner.

3 Read through the story of two British mountain climbers, Rachel Kelsey and Jeremy Colenso. Where were they? What went wrong? How were they saved? What does the text message mean?

4 Place the adverbs on the right of the story in the correct place in the same line (sometimes more than one place is possible). Add punctuation where necessary.

5 What background information are you given in the article? When does the actual story of what happened start?

6 Using the notes you made earlier, write the story of your dangerous experience (about 250 words).

- Begin with background information
- Describe the events in the order they happened.
- Make sure you use plenty of adverbs to describe people's feelings and actions.

Share your stories as a class, reading some of them aloud.

TEXTING TO THE RESCUE

On a mid-September day, British climbers Rachel Kelsey and Jeremy Colenso were climbing in the Swiss Alps.

They were both experienced climbers, and when they left their base, the weather was good. They reached the summit, but as they started the climb down, an electric storm struck the mountain. Snow began to fall, making it difficult to see where they could put their hands and feet on the rock. After several frightening minutes, they found a narrow ledge and climbed on to it, hoping the snow would stop and they could continue their descent.

The snow did not stop and the temperature dropped to −10°C. 'We had to stay awake,' said Rachel, 'because it was so cold that we would have died. So we told stories and rubbed our fingers and toes to keep them warm.'

They decided that they had to get help. But what could they do? Rachel had brought her mobile phone with her, but the only number contacts she had were in London. She sent a text message at 1.30 a.m. to get help. She sent the same text to five friends in the UK. It read: 'Need heli rescue off north ridge of Piz Badile, Switz'. They were all asleep, so nothing happened. At 5.00 a.m., one friend, Avery Cunliffe, got the message. He jumped into action, called the rescue services in Switzerland, and called Rachel to tell her that help was coming.

The weather was too bad for the helicopters to operate, but Avery kept sending text messages to the climbers. At about 10.00 p.m. they were lifted off the mountain. 'We owe our lives to Avery', they said when they were back at base.

several years ago
high / with great confidence

relatively
easily
suddenly / heavily / extremely
safely
gratefully / desperately

however / dangerously
afterwards / undoubtedly
continuously

eventually / possibly / fortunately
unfortunately

in fact
urgently
for hours / then
immediately
then

for the next 24 hours

finally / safely

exhaustedly

1 Use the conjunctions *but*, *although*, and *however* to join these two sentences.

She's rich and famous.   She's unhappy.

2 Conjunctions can join sentences to express **contrast**, **reason** and **result**, **time**, and **condition**. In each group complete the sentences with suitable conjunctions.

Contrast	however although despite even though

1 _____ I can't speak much Spanish, I can understand a lot.
2 I can't speak Spanish well. _____, I can understand most things.
3 He can't speak Spanish well, _____ he lives in Spain.
4 _____ living in Spain, he can't speak Spanish.

Reason and Result	such ... that so as since because so ... that

1 I didn't sleep well last night, _____ I'm tired.
2 I'm tired _____ I didn't sleep well last night.
3 I wanted to go, but _____ it was late, I decided not to.
4 _____ John can't be here today, I've been asked to chair the meeting.
5 He always looks _____ innocent _____ he gets away with murder.
6 He's _____ a terrible liar _____ no one believes him.

Time	when(ever) while as (soon as) until after since

1 I called you _____ I could.
2 He refused to talk to the police _____ his lawyer arrived.
3 I feel sad _____ I hear that song.
4 They were burgled _____ they were away on holiday.
5 I've known her _____ I was a small child.
6 I'll help you with this exercise _____ I've had dinner.

Condition	if as long as unless in case

1 _____ I'm going to be late, I'll call you.
2 You won't pass _____ you work harder.
3 Take an umbrella _____ it rains.
4 You can borrow my car _____ you drive carefully.

3 Discuss what you know about the film star, Marilyn Monroe.

4 Read about Marilyn's death and the conspiracy theories that surround it. Choose the correct conjunctions to join the sentences.

5 Research and write about someone famous who interests you. Use the plan below to help you.

Paragraph 1: Introduction and your interest in this person
Paragraph 2: Early life
Paragraph 3: Career path
Paragraph 4: Period of fame
Paragraph 5: Later life (and death)

MARILYN MONROE
THE DEATH OF A STAR

It is over 40 years (1) *since /after* Marilyn Monroe died, (2) *however /but* theories concerning her death still fascinate the world. (3) *Whenever /While* her name is mentioned, people recall the mystery of her final hours and (4) *although /despite* the official verdict was suicide, many believe that she was murdered by the Mafia or the FBI.

Marilyn had a reputation as a dumb blonde who had (5) *so /such* a problem with drink, drugs, and depression that she could never remember her lines. (6) *However /But*, her beauty and fame brought her into contact with some of the biggest names of the day. She dated Frank Sinatra, (7) *even though /despite* he had connections with the Mafia, and she also had affairs with President John Kennedy and his brother Bobby.

(8) *When /Until* Marilyn was found dead in bed at her home in Los Angeles in the early hours of Sunday, August 5, 1962, police assumed it was suicide (9) *but /as* there was an empty bottle of sleeping pills on the table beside her. (10) *Despite / However*, witnesses, including her psychiatrist and some of her friends, insisted she was not suicidal at the time. Other witnesses said they saw Bobby Kennedy visit her house that night, (11) *as long as / even though* he claimed to be in San Francisco. There were other suspicious events. Marilyn's housekeeper disappeared immediately (12) *after /since* she was found, only to reappear a year later as an employee of the Kennedys. Why would they employ her (13) *unless /if* they wanted her to keep silent? Marilyn's diaries also disappeared. Were they (14) *so /such* revealing that they had to be destroyed?

Marilyn's ex-husband Joe DiMaggio was convinced the Kennedys had her killed. He never spoke about it (15) *while /during* he was alive (16) *in case / unless* he also met an untimely death, but he did in his memoirs, which were published (17) *as soon as / since* he died.

1 How does writing an email differ from writing letters? List some differences.

2 Emails to friends are usually very informal and grammar words are often left out. How could you express these typical email phrases more formally?

> Glad you're OK.
> Great news – got the job!
> Sorry, can't make next Sat.
> You still OK for Friday?
> Thanks loads.
> Sounds fantastic.
> Can't wait to see you.
> Speak soon.

3 Read the email and note any features that are typical to emails. What changes would you make if it were a letter? Go through and discuss with your partner.

4 Read the letter from Jane to a friend. What is the main reason for writing? What parts of the letter give extra information?

Work with a partner and discuss how to make it more like an email.

5 Write an email in reply to Jane (about 250 words).

- Begin by reacting to her news
- Reply positively to her invitation
- Suggest arrangements for meeting her
- End by giving some news about yourself.

From: paul.gill@donawoo.es
Date: Tuesday 10 June, 5.36 pm
To: tonsar.holmes@btclick.com
Subject: Nice to see you in Cambridge

Hi Tony and Sarah

GREAT to see you in Cambridge last week and catch up on all your news. Wasn't the Old Church Hotel nice? (Hey, but what about the lousy breakfast service!). The party seemed to go OK. Wonder what the group photo will be like this year? Also, the bottle (or two!) of champagne in the bar after – MOST enjoyable!

Got back to Spain after a 2 day drive – stopped off at lovely 3 star hotel in village of Brioude on way to Montpellier. Kids loved the indoor pool and jacuzzi. Came as a welcome break from driving for us.

Hope all is well with you. Pam is off with kids to Aqualandia, swimming. Remember when we went up there with yours once – many moons ago?

Keep in touch. Would be great if you could get out here to visit us.

lots of love
Paul & Pam
& Hannah and Freddie

Wandsworth
London

July 8th

Dear Rob,

It was so good to see you and Jenny a few weeks ago. We really must get together more often, we always have so much to talk about.

On the subject of get-togethers, I just had a postcard from – guess who? Graham Pellowe. Do you remember 'gorgeous' Graham who was studying zoology? Well, he's in town. Apparently he's a real high-flier these days. He works for an international environmental agency, would you believe. Anyway, he's coming to London next Thursday and he really wants to meet up and discuss old times. He's staying with friends in Maida Vale, close to where I used to live. I know a great restaurant there called the Green Olive, or else there's the Red Pepper – both are excellent. Anyway, I am assuming and desperately hoping that you can come that evening – I don't fancy a whole evening with old Graham on my own. I finish work at about six and he can't make the restaurant until 8.30, which gives us some time to catch up. Let me know if any of this is possible.

Please call me or email when you can and I'll book the restaurant. It could be a fun evening.

Love
Jane

1 What do you understand by fast food? What fast food outlets are popular in your country? What do you understand by organic food? Do you ever buy it?

2 A company called the Organic Burger Company has commissioned a consumer survey to find out who their customers could be in the future. The results of the survey are presented to them as a report. Here are some headings from the report.

FAO (For the attention of ...)   ___
Title (of report)   ___
Background and objectives   ___ ___ ___
Research and findings   ___ ___ ___ ___
Summary and recommendations   ___ ___
Action next   ___ ___

Match these expressions with the headings.

a In conclusion,
b The Managing Director
c The purpose of this report
d two main findings
e The history of this issue
f 'Survey into Potential Demand for Organic Burgers.'
g We recommend that
h The results
i We propose that
j were asked to say what they thought
k within the next six months
l We were asked to investigate
m not enough evidence

3 Read the report based on the consumer survey conducted for the Organic Burger Company and complete it with the expressions from exercise 2.

The Organic Burger Company

FAO: (1)_____, Organic Burger Company
Title: (2)'_____'.
Date: 30th November

Background and objectives

(3)_____ is that there has recently been a drop in customers at traditional fast-food outlets such as McDonalds. The Organic Burger company wants to fill the growing gap in the market.

(4)_____ is to survey consumer attitudes by doing preliminary research with the young people of Nottingham, a medium-sized English town.

(5)_____ what the customers would want from the experience of buying and eating a high-quality organic burger.

Research and findings

We surveyed 120 people. The age range was:
16–19: 31%   **20–24:** 34%   **25–35:** 19%
36–50: 12%   **51+:** 4%

They (6)_____ about the following statements:

1 I prefer to eat organic meat in my burger.
                                    SA A DK D SD
2 I prefer to have a restaurant interior that is tasteful and modern.   SA A DK D SD
3 I prefer my food to be grown with respect for the environment.   SA A DK D SD
4 I prefer all the other ingredients to be fresh and organic.   SA A DK D SD
5 I am prepared to pay more than I pay now.
                                    SA A DK D SD

(SA = Strongly Agree, A = Agree,
DK = Don't Know, D = Disagree,
SD = Strongly Disagree)

(7)_____ are as follows:

1 **46%** agreed or strongly agreed
2 **47%** agreed or strongly agreed
3 **77%** agreed or strongly agreed
4 **39%** agreed or strongly agreed
5 **22%** agreed or strongly agreed

The (8)_____ are:

1. there is a growing preference for organic food.
2. there is (9)_____ that there is a large market yet.

Summary and recommendations

(10)_____ we believe that our survey showed that:

* the tastes of young people in a typical western town are changing
* demand exists for more stylish fast food and that this demand is growing.

(11)_____ the company loses no time in preparing for a push into all western markets.

Action next

(12)_____ further research is now carried out, on a larger scale and in other countries. This should be completed (13)_____.

WRITING A SURVEY AND A REPORT

4 You work for a firm of marketing consultants. Your client is a supermarket chain. Your brief is to find out if shoppers in your town would be prepared to buy more *Fairtrade* products in the local supermarket. *Fairtrade* products cost more, because they pay the producers in developing countries a better price for their products.

* Think of four or five statements like the ones used in the survey for the Organic Burger Company.

  I want to know where the things I buy come from.
  SA A DK D SD

* Ask at least 20 people, either in your class or outside your class.

* Take data about age. Possibly also male / female.

* Add up the statistics.

5 Write the report (about 250 words). Use expressions from exercises 2 and 3, and use the structure of the report as a model.

Tapescripts

UNIT 1

T 1.1

1 How long has Max been at summer camp?
Just two days.
2 Is he having a good time?
No, not really. He's feeling very homesick.
3 Is this his first time at summer camp?
No, it's not. He's been once before. Last year he went to Pine Trees.
4 Did he like it at Pine Trees?
Oh, yes he did, very much.
5 Why was that?
Because they did things like archery and mountain biking.
6 What's he doing tomorrow?
He's making pancakes.
7 Why does he want his cell phone?
Because all the other kids have theirs.

T 1.2

1 How long has Sophie been in New Zealand?
Nearly a week.
2 How long was she in Australia?
Three weeks.
3 Who is she travelling with?
Catherine.
4 Why does she like New Zealand?
Because it's smaller and cooler than Australia.
5 Why did she like Kangaroo Island?
Because of the wildlife. She saw some platypus there.
6 What's their car like?
It's OK – the lights work and it has a big glove box – but it sometimes makes strange noises.
7 Which wildlife has she seen already?
She's seen dolphins, whales, and enormous albatrosses.
8 Where are they going next?
They're heading up the west coast.
9 Why is she sending Rob photos?
So that he won't forget what she looks like.

T 1.3

1 A Are you being served, sir?
B Oh, -er, just looking, thank you.
2 I've heard that she's been seeing a lot of Patrick recently.
3 I'll be seeing Bill this afternoon – I'll tell him the good news then.
4 Apparently, he was overtaking on a bend at 70 mph when they stopped him.
5 I hadn't seen her since she was a little girl, and she'd changed beyond all recognition.
6 Nobody will listen to him. He's the kind of guy who isn't believed by anyone.
7 I haven't been told yet if I've got it. I'll be told in writing sometime next week.
8 Do you have any idea which address it was sent to?

T 1.4

1 A At weekends I often don't bother getting up 'til lunchtime.
B Absolutely! Why bother if you don't have to?
2 A My parents have never had a cross word in all their married lives.
B Really? Mine are at it all the time.
3 A I don't think I'll ever master this DVD player.
B Well, don't ask me. I can't even find the on/off button.
4 A I was saying to a friend just the other day that I hadn't seen you for ages.
B I know. How long has it been?

5 A I hate Mondays because nothing ever goes right on a Monday.
B Just Mondays, eh? Aren't you the lucky one!
6 A I'd just arrived home last night when I realized I'd left my briefcase on the bus.
B Well, you won't see that again.
7 A I was just getting ready to go out this morning when my grandmother rang for a chat. It's so frustrating!
B I know, and you feel really bad if you say it's not a good time.
8 A I've been told that our teacher wears purple pyjamas in bed!
B Who on earth told you that?!
9 A In my very first English lesson I was taught to introduce myself and say 'hello'.
B I was taught to say 'the cat runs after the mouse' and stuff like that – useful, uh?!
10 A The reason I'm learning English is because it's spoken all over the world.
B True. But isn't Chinese spoken by more people?

T 1.5

1 A Heard about Jane and John splitting up?
B No! Really? I always thought they got on really well.
A Apparently not. John's been seeing his ex-girlfriend.
2 A Leaving already? What's wrong?
B I just have a headache, that's all.
3 A Failed again? How many times is that?
B OK, OK. There's no need to rub it in! They say the *best* drivers fail three times.
4 A Sorry I'm late. Been waiting long?
B No, I've just arrived myself. Got caught in traffic.
5 A Doing anything interesting this weekend?
B Yeah, if you call housework interesting. I've just *got* to tidy my flat this weekend.
6 A Like the car! When did you get it?
B We've had it a while actually. Second-hand, you know.
7 A Bye, Jo! See you later.
B Yeah. I'll be round about eight!
8 A Just coming! Hang on!
B Get a move on, or we'll go without you!
9 A Want a lift? Hop in.
B Great. Can you drop me in the centre?
10 A Seen Jim lately?
B No, I haven't. I wonder what he's up to at the moment.

T 1.6 **A long-distance phone call**

D Hello?
K Dad! It's me, Kirsty.
D Kirsty! How are you? How's it all going?
K I'm fine, but still a bit jet-lagged.
D I can imagine. What exactly is the time difference over there?
K It's nine hours ahead. I just can't get used to it. Last night I lay awake all night and then today I nearly fell asleep at work in the middle of a meeting.
D You poor thing. And what's work like?
K It's early days but, I think it's going to be really good. It's a big company but everybody's being so kind and helpful. I've been trying to find out how everything works.
D And what about Tokyo? What's it like? Have you seen much of the city yet?
K I've seen a bit. It just seems such a big, busy city. I don't see how I'll ever find my way round it.
D I know. Big cities can seem really strange and frightening at first. Is it anything like London?
K No, it's nothing like London. It's like nowhere else I've ever been – masses of huge buildings,

underground shopping centres, lots of taxis and people – so many people – but it's so clean. No litter on the streets or anything.
D And where are you living? What kind of accommodation have you got?
K Well, for the time being I've been given a tiny apartment, but it's in a great part of town.
D What do you mean 'for the time being'? Will you be moving somewhere else?
K That's right. I won't be living here for long. I'll be offered a bigger place as soon as one becomes available, which is good 'cos this one really is tiny, but at least it's near to where I'm working.
D How do you get to work then? Do you walk?
K Walk! You're kidding. It's not *that* close. It's a short subway ride away. And the trains come so regularly – it's a really easy journey, which is good 'cos I start work very early in the morning.
D It all sounds really interesting but are you enjoying yourself?
K Again it's too early to say. I think I really will be enjoying it all soon. I'm sure it's going to be a great experience. It's just that I miss everyone at home so much.
D Oh, we miss you too, very much. Make sure you email us regularly – it's the best way to keep in touch.
K I will. I promise. And you email me back with all your news. I just love getting news from home. Give everyone my love. Bye.
D Bye sweetheart. It's been great talking to you.

T 1.7

1 A I'm going away on business for two weeks. Do you think you could possibly water my house plants for me?
B No problem. I'd be glad to. I'll keep an eye on your whole flat if you like.
A That would be great.
B Don't worry, I know how house-proud you are. I'll make sure everything stays clean and tidy.
A I'll do the same for you any time, you know.
B Thanks.
2 A Julie, have you heard? Anna's just been made managing director of the UK branch of her firm, so she's coming back from the States!
B Oh, that's great news. Let's give her a spectacular homecoming party when she gets back. Hmmm. She's certainly the career girl of the family.
A Doing really well, isn't she?
B I know and I'm happy for her. Me? I'm just a housewife. Four kids, home-made cakes and home-grown vegetables!
A And how *are* my wonderful grandchildren?
3 A We're having a house-warming party on the 12th. Can you come?
B Yes, you bet. We'd love to! But I didn't know you'd moved.
A Yeah, two weeks ago. It's much bigger than the old one. Huge kitchen and three big bedrooms.
B Sounds great.
A Yeah. Mind you, there's much more housework to do!
B That's a drag!
4 A Hey, you going to Carly's on Saturday?
B I dunno.
A It's a free house. It'll be great.
B Cool. Where are her parents then?
A Carly says they're visiting her grandma – she's sick and housebound so they have to go and help.
B OK. Count me in. I'll be there.

1 I'm going away for two weeks. Do you think you could possibly water my house plants for me?
2 Don't worry, I know how house-proud you are. I'll make sure everything stays clean and tidy.
3 Let's give her a spectacular homecoming party when she gets back from New York.
4 Me? I'm just a housewife. Four kids, home-made cakes and home-grown vegetables!
5 We're having a house-warming party on the 12th. Can you come? I'll give you our new address.
6 Mind you, with it being much bigger, there's much more housework to do!
7 Her grandmother's sick and housebound so they have to go and help.

T 1.9 **Things I miss from home**

Andrew

Well, the thing I miss most when I'm away from home is definitely listening to the radio, and the way I get round this, particularly when I go away for two, three or four months or something, is to take a small short wave radio that I found and take great trouble to tune in this short wave radio to get an English language station, something like the World Service. And I'm there, waving the aerial around and twiddling the knob, and trying to find the correct kind of station, but then suddenly when it all comes in, and you can hear it, it's great, it really makes me feel like I'm back home, back in my bedroom tuning into weird programmes on wonderful subjects really.

Helen

When I'm away from home for any length of time, something that I really have to have with me is my hair straighteners, … erm … I can't bear to wake up in the morning and be without them, because my hair is most unruly, and I would feel very uncomfortable having gone out without straightening my hair beforehand, so I have to take those with me whenever I stay with friends or go on holiday.

Gabriele

When I'm away for a little bit longer, … erm … what I do miss are my two cats and I do take a photo of them. That sounds very silly but I like to see them from time to time.

Paul

Erm … if I'm away from home for a while, what I usually miss most is my bed. I like a good solid bed. Er … in particular what I find I miss if I'm in a hotel is a pillow that I like. I do find that hotels have this incredible knack of providing pillows that you just can't sleep with – there always seems to be two pillows on the bed and if you use one it's never enough, and if you use both of the pillows, your head seems to be just stuck up in the air – so I have thought of taking a pillow with me but that seems a bit excessive. Erm … but again connected with sleep, one thing I always do take with me is ear plugs. I find they're absolutely invaluable, if you're not sure where you're going to be in a hotel and if it's very noisy, as long as you're quite used to sleeping with ear plugs … er … they can be wonderful 'cause you don't need to worry about traffic and people making a lot of noise in the next room.

Sylvia

Well, when I'm away from home … erm … there are several things I miss, the usual ones, my children of course, and a good cup of tea … erm … but something I realize I do miss is, is the news, and it's not, it's not that other countries don't have any news, but I'm very attached to a particular news programme and a particular presenter, and if they're not around to tell me the news, I can't quite believe it. It's very odd – doesn't happen with papers, I'm happy to read another paper but on the telly I like to see, I like to see a familiar face and … erm … the same background colours and it's all very reassuring, even if he's telling something dreadful. But what do I take … erm … with me? I always travel with a bag of snacks, … erm … I don't know why, because I'm terr… er … I'm just terrified of, of being hungry while I'm travelling and not finding anything I want to eat. Gosh, I didn't, I didn't think I was so fussy – there you go!

Chris

I think the thing I miss most when I go away for an extended period, on holiday or whatever … er … especially if I go away abroad is probably Sunday morning, and by that I really mean a lazy Sunday morning when I can get up fairly late, wander down to the newsagent's, buy the newspaper, come back with a croissant and make a big pot of coffee, and spend … er … at least the morning and maybe a large part of the day just sitting around reading the paper, drinking coffee and relaxing.

T 1.10

1 A Great to see you. Come on in.
   B I was just passing and thought I'd drop in.
2 A Excuse me, don't I know you from somewhere?
   B No, I don't think so.
3 A What d'you mean you're not coming?
   B Well, I just don't feel up to going out tonight.
4 A I think I'll have the chocolate mousse. What about you?
   B Let me see. No, actually, I don't think I'll bother with dessert.
5 A My flatmate can't make it to your party.
   B Really! That's a drag. I was hoping to meet her.
6 A How come you're not having a holiday this year?
   B We just can't afford it.
7 A You'll make yourself ill if you carry on working at that pace.
   B That's as maybe but I have to get this finished by Friday.
8 A I've got you the last two tickets for the show.
   B Fantastic! I knew you'd swing it for us.

T 1.11 See p15

T 1.12 See p89

T 1.13

1 A Excuse me, don't I know you from somewhere?
   B Actually, I don't think so.
   A Weren't you at Gavin's party last week?
   B Not me. I don't know anyone called Gavin.
   A Well, someone who looked just like you was there.
   B Well, that's as maybe but it certainly wasn't me.
   A I am sorry!
2 A Tony! Hi! Great to see you.
   B Well, I was just passing and I thought I'd drop in and say 'hello'.
   A Come on in! Have a drink!
   B You're sure? You're not too busy?
   A Never too busy to talk to you.
   B Thanks Jo. It'd be really nice to have a chat.
   A Fantastic! Let me take your coat.

UNIT 2

T 2.1 **Marco Polo 1254–1324**

Marco Polo was the first person to travel the entire 8,000 kilometre length of the Silk Route, the main trade link between Cathay (China) and the West for over two thousand years. He was born in Venice, the son of a merchant. In 1271, when he was 17, he set off for China. The journey took him four years. His route led him through Persia, Afghanistan, and Mongolia. He travelled by boat, but mainly on horseback, and he frequently got lost. He was met by the emperor Kublai Khan. He was one of the first Europeans to visit the territory, and he travelled extensively. He went over mountain ranges, down rivers, and across deserts. He stayed in China for seventeen years. When he left, he took back a fortune in gold and jewellery. He arrived back home in 1295. He wrote a book called *The Travels of Marco Polo*, which gave Europeans their first information about China and the Far East.

Tommy Willis, backpacker in Asia

Tommy Willis is in Fiji. He's on a nine-month backpacking trip round south-east Asia. He flew into Bangkok five months ago. Since then, he's been to Vietnam, Hong Kong, South Korea, and Japan. He's visited royal palaces and national parks in South Korea, and climbed to the summit of Mount Fuji in Japan. He's been staying in cheap hostels, along with a lot of other young people. 'I've met a lot of really great people, but it hasn't all been easy,' said Tommy. 'I've had diarrhoea a few times, and I've been pickpocketed once. I've also been mugged, which was really scary.' Apart from that, his only worry is the insects. He's been stung all over his body. He's been travelling mainly by public transport – bus, train, and ferry, but when he's been able to afford it, he's also taken the occasional plane. He's looking forward to taking things easy for another week, then setting off again for Australia. 'Once you've got the travel bug, it becomes very hard to stay in the same place for too long,' he said.

T 2.2

He's been stung all over his body.
He's visited royal palaces.
He's been staying in cheap hostels.
I've been pickpocketed and mugged.
I've met a lot of really great people.
He's been to Vietnam and Japan.

T 2.3

1 When and where was he born?
   In 1254 in Venice.
2 How long did it take to travel to China?
   Four years.
3 How long did he stay in China?
   For seventeen years.
4 What did he take back to Venice?
   Gold and jewellery.
5 What was his book called?
   The Travels of Marco Polo.
6 How long has he been away from home?
   For five months.
7 Which places has he been to?
   Thailand, Vietnam, Hong Kong, South Korea, and Japan.
8 Where's he been staying?
   In cheap hostels.
9 How many times has he had diarrhoea?
   A few times.
10 Has he been pickpocketed?
   Yes, once.

T 2.4

1 **Alan**

They are … one of the most eerie … and -er strange experiences you can possibly have. The first time I saw them, they appeared as a kind of shimmering curtain, over the top of a ridge of mountains, and they went from a greeny colour to a kind of purply red colour. And they just stayed there. The second time I saw them, it was the most amazing sight because they were right above our heads, and they covered the whole of the sky. The other interesting thing is that -er not everybody hears it, but they sometimes make a sound, a kind of -er buzzing noise. It was a real sense of wonder and awe. I just kind of sat there with my mouth hanging open, just feeling kind of small.

2 **James**

You start at the bottom of the valley, and slowly make your way up the hill, -er about a seven-hour hike until you get to a camp. Then you get up very early the next morning, about four o'clock, in order to get there for the sunrise. You walk for an hour or so, and suddenly you reach this point where you're looking down on this ancient city, just as the sun is breaking through the clouds. It's the most extraordinary sight. And you walk around in the total silence of a city that's more than five hundred years old. At that point it's invaded by thousands of tourists, and -er it's time to go.

3 Willow
We got up about five o'clock in the morning. We went to the site, and set off. Because you're floating with the wind, there is no breeze on you, and it really was like ... flying like a bird. You could look down on everyone, and they were all so small, like ants. It was just amazing, and so silent. And we landed about seven o'clock, and suddenly we were back with the rest of civilization. It was just the most beautiful experience.

T 2.5
1 When you go for a job interview, it's important to make a good impression.
2 I think we're all getting tired. Can I make a suggestion? How about a break?
3 A lot of research has been done into the causes of cancer.
4 I think the director is basically doing a good job. He's reliable, he's honest, and he gets results.
5 I'd like to make it clear right now that I am totally opposed to this idea.
6 Right. I think we should make a start and get down to business.
7 I don't mind if we go now or later. It makes no difference to me.
8 Could you do me a favour and lend me some money till tomorrow?

T 2.6
1 I'm so thirsty. I could do with a cup of tea.
2 We've bought an old flat. We're going to do it up over the next few years.
3 I think we should do away with the monarchy. They're all useless. And expensive.
4 I could never do without my personal assistant. She organizes everything for me.

T 2.7
1 Thieves broke into the castle and made off with jewellery and antique paintings.
2 Jake's parents buy him loads of toys. They're trying to make up for always being at work.
3 What do you make of the new boss? I quite like him.
4 You didn't believe his story, did you? He made the whole thing up.

T 2.8   Tashi Wheeler – girl on the move

I = Interviewer, T = Tashi
Part one
I Now, travelling. Erm ... when did you start travelling?
T When I was eight months old.
I And where did you go?
T Erm I think we did a lot of South ... yeah we did a lot of South East Asia when I was younger. And Galapagos Islands, Philippines, and stuff like that.
I And your first memories ... OK, eight months, you started, but you presumably don't ...
T ... don't remember.
I What are your first memories of travelling?
T Erm ... airports. Erm ... what else? Beaches. It was a lot in Asia at the time, so it was always hot. Big fruit drinks, and ... I don't know, lots of bus rides.
I Was there a time at which you sort of felt 'Yeah, I quite enjoy this travelling', or was it ...? It sounds almost a bit of a chore, the way you describe it at the moment.
T No, it was never a chore. I always really enjoyed it. I think I was quite comfortable. Mum used to say that when I was two years old she just put me down and I just ran off. And she wouldn't see me

and then someone would pick me up and bring me back. I was quite happy fitting in everywhere.
I What do you think were your, your best memories of travelling? I mean, what can you actually remember that still stands out years on?
T From when I was much younger?
I Yes.
T Erm ... Africa, when I think I was around eight, or nine. We had ... we went on safaris there, and got chased by an elephant, had lion cubs jumping around the ... erm ... safari bus, monkeys swinging off the ... erm ... rear-view mirrors, and things. So that was ... and trekking in Nepal is something I'll always remember. The getting up at like four in the morning and looking over all the mountains, and then just walking all day, talking to porters, and coming into villages, and all the kids running out and seeing you, and things. There's lots of amazing experiences.

T 2.9   Part two
I And when you were on these travels, I mean, did your Dad sort of have a notebook, and he'd be sort of stopping everywhere ...?
T Constantly.
I ... and writing detailed notes of everywhere?
T Yeah, he's always got pen and paper and three or four guidebooks and other people's guidebooks and so on.
I And that must have made travelling a lot slower for you as a family.
T Oh, no. He's hectic, Dad. He's ... We land in a country, his feet hit the ground, and he takes off. We don't stop for two seconds. He gets up and goes out before we get up, comes back, gets us up, takes us to breakfast, we rush around all the sights, see everything, stop for one drink here, lunch somewhere else, dinner somewhere else, after dinner drink somewhere else, takes us back to the hotel and he goes out again, and goes on all night.
I Amazingly exhausting!
T Ah, it is! It's really exhausting! It got to a point where me and my brother ... what we really liked about travelling for a while was sitting at home watching movies and getting room service. That was quite exciting and different for us.
I This raises the question, of course, travel broadening the mind, as ... as ... is often said. Do you think it does?
T Yeah, definitely. I don't think you can travel and not have your mind broadened. We saw everything, we ran around, and it was hectic, but at the same time, you knew it was an experience while you were doing it, especially as you got older. And you value it. And still do.

T 2.10   Part three
I I was going to say, we've talked a bit about, you know, when you were really young. What about as you got older? I mean, how did the sort of experience and feel of it change, as you became say a teenager, and ... mid-teenage years and so on?
T You always wanted to stay home, summer holidays. I mean, just before you go away ... there'd be all your friends having parties and holidays and things, and you'd want to stay and hang out. But at the same time you knew you were doing something different, and everyone's always asking you about where you've been, and what you're doing, so you know you ... it's a privileged situation, and you're lucky to have it.
I Did that make it easier for you socially, or ... or not so easy?
T Erm ...
I Being different in that way, in that you'd travelled sort of more than anyone, really, hadn't you?
T I think it had its pros and cons. I think for a number of years, especially around probably thirteen to sixteen, I felt backward, I think, 'cos I didn't really know how to get along with kids my age and my own culture and country and stuff. Erm ... just from travelling for so long in places,

countries, cultures or whatever, where you can't talk to boys, or you can't look at people in a certain way, or you don't wear certain clothing, or something. And I think ... I don't know ... just the adjusting back and forth constantly did make it a little awkward. The kids at school seemed to be cool, and they had things going on, watch TV, and this programme was good, and I was never up to date with all that stuff, so I was constantly being pulled out of it and brought back. But at the same time, I did have that, like I'd seen things, I knew things, and stuff – just a broader view of life I guess.
I There is a view of travelling that you become a kind of world citizen, and the world is your home.
T Melbourne's definitely my home. But I do feel comfortable anywhere, particularly in Asia, I don't know ... I think I'm a real ... I just feel like I'm coming home when I go back to Asia. And after living for a year in Paris, I love going back there, but it's not really my home, I guess. No, Melbourne is definitely my home.
I Is there anywhere you fe... don't feel comfortable?
T Erm ... I haven't found that place yet! But you never know, I might. I haven't been everywhere.
I Your mother's not so long ago written a book about travelling with children, hasn't she? Is travelling ... would ... is that, is that something you'd sort of advocate, travelling with children? Would you travel with ... will you travel with your own children?
T Yeah, definitely. I think ... I mean ... it's a time where your ideas, your personality is being formed, and I think ... it can only benefit you. Really. I think it's something ... And you don't have as much time to do these things when you're older, so try to fit as much of it in as you can when you're younger. Definitely.
I So you'll continue travelling yourself, will you, do you think?
T I hope so. I really can't handle being in one place for too long. I get very itchy-footed.

T 2.11
1 How's your steak? Is it OK?
2 We were all going on holiday to Spain next week. We were really looking forward to it, but my father's been quite ill so we had to cancel the holiday.
3 **A** Has Ann had the baby yet? It must be due any time now.
   B Oh, yes. Haven't you heard? She didn't have one baby. She had three! Tom's the father of triplets!
4 Mind your head as you come through this door. It's very low.
5 Do be careful. That bowl's really heavy.
6 Did you know that they eat horse-meat in some countries? And snails. And pigs' feet.
7 Look! Isn't that Peter over there, sitting on his own?
8 Sarah told me that she hated me. She said that you never wanted to see me ever again!
9 I saw Julie yesterday.
10 Tomorrow's test has been cancelled!

T 2.12
1 **A** How's your steak? Is it OK?
   B Mmm! It's absolutely delicious! Just the way I like it.
2 **A** We were all going on holiday to Spain next week. We were really looking forward to it, but my father's been quite ill, so we had to cancel the holiday.
   B Ah! What a shame! You must be so disappointed!
3 **A** Has Ann had the baby yet? It must be due any time now.
   B Oh, yes. Haven't you heard? She didn't have one baby. She had three! Tom's the father of triplets!
   A Wow! That's unbelievable! How amazing! Triplets! That'll keep them busy!

4 A Mind your head as you come through this door. It's very low.

B Ouch! That really hurt!

A I told you! Well, it isn't bleeding, but you'll have a nice bruise.

5 A Do be careful. That bowl's really heavy.

B Whoops! Sorry about that! I dropped it! Don't worry. I'll get you a new one.

6 A Did you know that they eat horse-meat in some countries? And snails. And pigs' feet.

B Yuk! That's disgusting! You wouldn't catch me eating that!

7 A Look! Isn't that Peter over there, sitting on his own?

B Hey, Peter! Come over here and sit with us. Let's have a chat.

8 A Sarah told me that you hated me. She said that you never wanted to see me ever again!

B Uh? That's nonsense! What a stupid thing to say! You know it's not true.

9 A I saw Julie yesterday.

B Oh, really? How interesting! I haven't seen her for ages. How is she?

10 A Tomorrow's test has been cancelled.

B Phew! What a relief! Thank goodness for that! I hadn't done any revising for it at all.

T 2.13 See p25

T 2.14

1 I've just won $25,000 on the lottery!
2 Let's have a long coffee break!
3 Maria, you wrote 'at Rome' instead of 'in Rome'.
4 We were stuck in a traffic jam for four hours!
5 Look at the state of the kitchen! It hasn't been cleaned for weeks!
6 Rain, rain, rain.
7 The teacher told us to learn the dictionary for homework!
8 We hadn't heard from our daughter for a month, then she phoned last night.
9 My sister says it's possible to learn French in three months!
10 Yesterday I got a tax bill for $20,000.

UNIT 3

T 3.1

1 A Did you read that story about the guy who went over the Niagara Falls?

B No. What happened to him? Did he die?

A No, he survived, amazingly enough.

B Really? But I suppose he was wearing some kind of protection.

A That's the incredible thing. He was just wearing ordinary clothes. He just jumped in, fell down 180 feet, and somehow managed to avoid hitting the rocks.

B That's amazing! What did he do it for?

A Apparently he just did it for a dare. He'd been talking about doing it for ages. His friends had bet him he wouldn't do it.

B What a crazy guy!

A You're not kidding. The strange thing is, before he jumped, people around him said he'd been smiling.

B Wow! How weird!

2 A There was this story the other day about ... this woman mountain climber ...

B Uh huh. What about her?

A Well, she was stuck on top of a mountain, and she only managed to escape by sending text messages.

B Gosh! Where did this happen?

A In the Swiss Alps, I think. She was climbing with a partner. They'd been climbing for three hours when they got trapped in a terrible storm.

B You're kidding!

A No. But they built a shelter or something, and they hid in that.

B Then what happened?

A She started sending text messages to friends in London, and one of them sent a text back saying that the mountain rescue teams in Switzerland had been contacted.

B Uh huh.

A They tried to find them, but the weather was too bad – storms and everything.

B Oh, no!

A Anyway, they were rescued the next night, and now they're safe and sound.

B Thank goodness for that!

3 A I was reading in the paper the other day about a schoolboy who hacked into the United States military computers.

B No! Really? How old was he? 17? 18?

A Actually he was only 14.

B How did he do it?

A Well, he'd developed his own software program, and he'd been using this to download films and music from the Internet.

B I don't get it. What's that got to do with the US military?

A Well, he'd figured that if he broke into these powerful military computers, he could use them to download stuff even faster, so he wasn't really trying to get to their secrets.

B Oh, I see. I bet they were worried, though.

A They were. They got in touch with Scotland Yard, and this boy was tracked down to his house in North London.

B And he's only 14! They should give him a job!

T 3.2

He was wearing ordinary clothes.
He'd been talking about doing it for ages.
His friends had bet him he wouldn't do it.
She was climbing with a partner.
They were rescued the next night.

T 3.3

This is the six o'clock news.
Ten workers have been rescued from an accident 400 feet beneath the streets of London. They had spent the past 36 hours trapped underground. They had been digging a tunnel for a new Underground line when the roof collapsed. Sixty men managed to escape immediately, but two were fatally injured. Last night the ten men were recovering in hospital. An investigation into the cause of the accident is due to start tomorrow.

T 3.4

Three children who had been missing for two days have been found safe and well. The three ten-year-olds, two boys and a girl, disappeared after school on Wednesday. Police had issued photographs of the three, and had been searching nearby houses. They were eventually spotted by a neighbour, who alerted the police. They said they had slept out in a garden shed for a dare, and hadn't realized the concern they had caused.

T 3.5 Books and films

Paul

Certainly one of my favourite films is *Witness*. It's the one starring Harrison Ford, where he plays a detective who's investigating a murder that an Amish child has witnessed, and he has to protect the child and to do that at one point he has to go and spend some time living with the Amish community. Now the Amish community are that religious group ... erm ... in America who live a very old-fashioned lifestyle. They have no modern gadgets and no modern technology because their religion doesn't allow it. Now, Harrison Ford plays this very tough, hard-nosed city cop and there are some wonderful scenes where his values and culture really clash with

this very peaceful Amish community. It's also, it has a love story in it because he falls in love with the boy's mother, who's Amish. It's a very, very intense and passionate love story, and it's a thriller because it deals with police corruption, and it's unbearably tense and the build up towards the end is incredible. It really, really does have you on the edge of your seat.

Kate

I don't know if I'd say this is my favourite book, but this is certainly a book that made ... erm ... quite an impression on me. The book is called ... erm ... *The Secret History* and it's by Donna Tartt, and ... erm ... without actually giving away entirely what happens in the story, ... erm ... *The Secret History* is about a group of students and it's all about somebody's desire to belong to a group. And in fact the group of students ... erm ... do something really, really terrible. Erm ... they are involved in a murder and you know right from the beginning of the novel that this is going to happen and so you would think that there isn't any element of suspense because you know that somebody's going to die and you have some idea about how they're actually going to die, but in fact ... erm ... the whole story's very, very claustrophobic. You feel sort of trapped inside the group and trapped inside their situation. It's completely compelling to read. It's not a comfortable read but it was about 600 pages long and I read it in about a week ... erm ... and I lived and breathed this book over that week. Erm ... I would recommend it to anybody who wants to read something that psychologically is really dramatic.

T 3.6 The money jigsaw

I = Interviewer, R = Rachel

I Well and one of those girls, Rachel Aumann, is on the line now as we speak. Good morning to you, Rachel.

R Good morning.

I Erm ... extraordinary, this. You saw these bits of bank notes just blowing in the wind?

R Yeah, it was ... erm ... like really out of the ordinary. We were just walking to school and there's ripped up notes flying all over the floor. And then we traced it to like a bin, so that's where the ... the big bag was full of them.

I How big a bag?

R Erm ...

I Like a bin bag or something?

R No, actually, not that big ... erm ... it's about, I think it was like a Sainsbury's bag, like one of those.

I And it was just jammed full of torn-up banknotes, what fivers and tenners and that sort of thing?

R Yeah, just fives, tens, twenties.

I And how little were the pieces?

R Erm ... some were bigger than stamp sizes.

I That small though?

R Yeah, some were smaller.

I And so what did you do? You took them to the police or something?

R Erm we, we had to go to school so we went to school and then ... erm ... after school we were playing outside around ... erm ... like on the same road and ... erm ... when the police arrived we were, we went over then and started talking to them and telling them when we found it.

I And they took them away at that stage, did they?

R Yeah.

I And then what happened?

R Erm ... they kept them for like a long time 'cos there's a certain amount of months that they have to keep them before you, they can give them back.

I Right.

R And I think they went to the Royal Bank of England and to Scotland Yard and ... erm ... when ... erm ... they said yeah, it's real money ... erm ... they gave it back and we put it together.

I You say you put it together, but tiny bits of bank notes it must have taken you forever to do ... I mean, what a jigsaw puzzle!

R Yeah it's taken ages 'cos it's been about a year and we still haven't finished.

I So how many have you got left now then?

R Erm ... we have all the fives to do and just a few twenties but the tens are all finished.

I Extraordinary! Is it ... how much time do you spend doing this?

R Erm ... well when we first got it we did like half an hour, an hour a day but then as like time passed we just slowly like died down and didn't do as much.

I But I'm trying to picture you doing this. What do you do, do you stick bits of sellotape or something, or do you stick them onto a piece of paper or what?

R Well you have to get, you get the two serial numbers and ... erm ... then you have to get like a little bit from the middle of the note and so once you've got that, you just put sticky tape on the back of them so that they all stay together and put it in a bag.

I Good heavens! And you're going to carry on doing it, eh?

R Yeah, hopefully.

I £1200 so far?

R Erm ... yeah.

I And how much do you reckon you will be worth at the end of it all?

R Erm ... I think we if stick to it we could probably get about £2,000.

I Well, I think that you've earned every penny of it, Rachel. Thank you very much.

R Thank you.

T 3.7

A Jade's got a new boyfriend.

B A new boyfriend? Good for her!

A Apparently, he lives in a castle.

B Does he? How amazing!

A Yes. She met him in Slovenia.

B In Slovenia? That's interesting.

A Unfortunately, he can't speak much English.

B Can't he? I thought everyone could these days!

T 3.8 See p33

T 3.9

1 **A** Sam wants to apologize.
　B Does he?
　A Yes. He's broken your mother's Chinese vase.
　B My mother's Chinese vase? Oh, no!

2 **A** We had a terrible holiday.
　B Did you?
　A Yes. It rained all the time.
　B Did it?
　A Yes. And the food was disgusting!
　B Was it? What a drag!

3 **A** I'm broke.
　B Are you? How come?
　A Because I just had a phone bill for £500.
　B £500? Why so much?
　A Because I have a girlfriend in Korea.
　B Do you? How interesting!

4 **A** It took me three hours to get here.
　B Did it?
　A Yes. There was a traffic jam ten miles long.
　B Ten miles long? That's awful!
　A Now I've got a headache!
　B Have you? Poor darling. I'll get you something for it.

5 **A** I'm on a mountain, watching the sun set.
　B Are you?
　A Yes. And I've got something very important to ask you.
　B Have you? What is it? I can't wait!
　A You'd better sit down. I'd like to marry you.
　B Marry me? Wow!

UNIT 4

T 4.1

1 Oh dear! It's not that I *dislike* him, I just don't *love* him. How can I tell him I don't want to marry him without hurting his feelings? Trouble is, I actually fancy his best friend!

2 There's this group of lads you see – they're always chasing me and I don't think it's for fun. But I can't tell my mum and dad – if they find out, they'll go to the head teacher and complain and that would make everything much worse.

3 How do you tell someone when they look awful? That dress doesn't suit her at all. But I don't know how to tell her. She obviously thinks she looks great in it.

4 Me and Emma are going clubbing, but I daren't tell my Dad – he'd kill me. I've got an important exam next week and I haven't done a thing for it. I haven't a clue when I'll be back.

5 I know I'm not really ill. But it's a beautiful day and I don't want to sit in a stuffy office all day. I'm off to play golf. I never have days off usually.

6 I don't care who it is. I had a late night and I feel really rough this morning. Tell them I'm in an important meeting and I don't want be disturbed at the moment.

T 4.2

1 Who did she give it to?
2 What do you want to have a word about?
3 Who did you dance with?
4 What do you need it for?
5 Who did you get it from?
6 Who did you buy it for?
7 What are you thinking about?
8 Where do you want a lift to?

T 4.3 See p36

T 4.4

1 **A** Don't you like ice-cream?
　B No. I know it's weird, but I never have done. Not even vanilla.

2 **A** Don't you like learning English?
　B No, actually, I don't. I think it's really difficult.

3 **A** Don't you like your neighbours?
　B Well, they're all right, but they make a lot of noise.

4 **A** Haven't you ever been abroad?
　B Not really. I went to Scotland once, but that's not really abroad, is it?

5 **A** Haven't you got a TV at home?
　B No. We must be the only people in the whole world without a telly.

6 **A** Isn't it Tuesday today?
　B Yeap. It follows on from Monday.

7 **A** Isn't this your pen?
　B No, it isn't, actually. Mine's blue. That's black.

8 **A** Didn't you go to the States last year?
　B You bet. All down the east coast from Boston to Florida.

9 **A** Aren't you going to the races next weekend?
　B Uh huh. And I bet I'll lose a fortune. Hey ho!

T 4.5 My mate Norman

Part one
My mate Norman's a funny guy. He's an insomniac, he's dyslexic, and he's an atheist. He's single, unemployed, and lives all alone in a tiny one-roomed flat without even a pet for company. Also he's vegetarian and teetotal. He's -er pretty anti-social, actually.

Part two
I went round to see him last Sunday. As I walked up the drive, his dog started barking. His wife answered the door, and she called for Norman to come downstairs and join us in the living room. He was in a bad mood because he'd overslept that morning

and he'd been late for church. He also had a bit of an hangover, which he told me was the result of a wild party that they'd had at his house the night before. All his friends from his office were there. They'd had a barbecue in the garden with steaks and burgers. One of his favourite pastimes is doing crosswords, and while he was talking to me, he was doing one of those big puzzles from the newspaper.
'So how are you, Norman?' I asked him.
'KO, mate, KO. How about you?'
Anyway, as I said, Norman's an insomniac, dyslexic, atheist. So the joke is that he lies awake all night wondering about the existence of dog. Get it?

T 4.6 My most memorable lie

1 Andrew
Well, one lie I can remember from when I was younger was when, with a friend in the basement of my house, we were playing pool, 'cos we had a pool table down there, and decided to smoke our first cigarettes, these fantastic gold-filtered cigarettes, I remember – quite expensive – and halfway through the second or third cigarette, my dad came home, who was very anti-smoking, and we stubbed out our cigarettes and pushed them through a kind of grate underneath the window and he found them about a day later and he asked me if these, you know, if I knew what these cigarette stubs were all about, if I'd been smoking, and I completely denied all knowledge of these cigarettes and in fact pool, and the basement, and everything else.

2 Paul
I have one memory of regularly lying as a child and ironically it was to a priest, which sounds a bit alarming, but … erm … I was brought up Catholic and from the age of seven you had to go to confession every week and confess your sins and when you're that age, … erm … first of all you're not quite sure what a proper sin is, and also you just can't remember, and every week you had to go in and, and tell the priest some sins that you'd committed, so of course it's, it's quite common that what you end up doing is just making things up … erm … you say, 'I swore and I stole some biscuits from the pantry in the kitchen …' and bizarrely what you end up doing is lying to the priest so that you've got something to say in your confession.

3 Carolyn
I can think of a, a time recently when I had to tell a white lie which was … erm … basically when a friend of mine got married. Erm … it, they actually got married in America because his wife's American, so I didn't go to the wedding but they, they were showing me the photos and … erm … basically she looked absolutely awful she had a really horrible dress on that really did nothing for her figure and didn't suit her at all and just looked much older than she really is and quite frumpy, but … erm … yes obviously you can't say that when you see someone's wedding pictures, so I said 'that's really pretty, you look really lovely'. I felt really horrible as a result.

4 Kiki
One lie I can remember telling was when I lost a necklace that my grandmother had made for me especially – it had a 'K' on it. And I know where I lost it, I lost it at a party because … erm … I was having a very good time and wasn't taking care of it and I lied and told her it had been stolen in a robbery we had at our house. And to this day I've never told her what happened to it. But sometimes when she mentions things like 'Ooh I should get you another one', … er … it comes back to me.

5 Sean
The first lie I can really remember … erm … was – when I was at school. I must have been about five or six years old and I was in the playground and I was just about to get into a fight and … erm … the only way I could think of defending myself was to say … erm … 'You can't hit me, I go to judo lessons'. Erm … and I don't know where it came from, I'd never done

judo in my life and ... erm ... I wasn't even sure what judo was, but people left me alone ... erm ... because they thought I did judo. Erm ... but then people started to take an interest, they asked me where I went, and when the lessons were, how much they cost, and ... erm ... eventually somebody's mother rang my mother to get details of, of these judo lessons, which was when I had to admit that it was all, it was all a lie and ... erm ... it was a bit embarrassing really.

6 Kate

I do remember ... erm ... possibly the first time I, I told a lie as a child because it had some rather unpleasant consequences ... erm ... this happened when I was about ... er ... maybe four or five years old, and I had been ... erm ... playing with the dressing-up box that we had in our children's playroom, which was an enormous box full of wonderful ... erm ... clothes, and you could be a princess, you could be a soldier, you could be whatever, whatever you found in the dressing up box. And I was playing with our pet cat, and I put him in the box, and I left him there, and I shut the lid for hours and hours and hours and – I was four or five, I forgot about him – and I went off and did something else and didn't think any more of it, and when my mother asked after the cat, ... erm ... struck with horror, I lied and, and said that I hadn't seen him, and I hadn't played with him, and I probably said 'and I didn't put him in the dressing-up box' because my mother went and found him, and I do remember telling this lie because I was spanked for it.

T 4.7

1 A Gary's a really successful businessman.
  B Yeah, but he's a complete failure as a family man. He never sees his children.
2 A My grandad's so generous he gives me £20 every time I see him.
  B Lucky you! My grandad's famous for his meanness. A fiver every birthday, *if* he remembers.
3 A Well, Henry, I'm pleased there's been some improvement in your behaviour this term ... but sadly your work has got worse.
  B Didn't I do OK in the test then?
4 A You're not going bungee-jumping! It sounds really dangerous.
  B No, honestly, it's safe enough as long as you're careful.
5 A Our teacher is always criticizing us. I feel useless.
  B I know – it's not fair, he should give us more encouragement if he wants us to work hard.

T 4.8

1 A What a boring party!
  B You're right, it wasn't exactly an exciting evening.
2 A I don't know about you, but I thought the holiday was awful.
  B Well, it wasn't the most fun I've had.
3 A I can't believe how mean Jane is!
  B Mmmm, I suppose she's not famous for her generosity.
4 A That was one helluva difficult exam! I couldn't do a thing.
  B Too right, I've seen easier papers.

T 4.9

1 I'm sorry to bother you, but could you possibly change a ten-pound note?
  Have you got change for a ten-pound note?
2 Where's the station?
  Could you tell me where the station is, please?
3 A This is a present for you.
  B For me! Oh, how kind! You shouldn't have, really. Thank you so much.
  C This is a present for you.
  D Thanks.

4 A Can you come to a party on Saturday?
  B No, I can't.
  C Can you come to a party on Saturday?
  D Oh, what a pity! I'm already going out, I'm afraid.
  C Oh well, never mind!
  D But, thanks for the invitation anyway.
5 A Excuse me! Do you mind if I sit down here?
  B No, not at all.
  C Is anyone sitting here?
  D No.
6 A Can you give me a hand? I need to carry this box upstairs.
  B OK, if you like.
  C I wonder if I could possibly ask you a favour? Would you mind helping me with this box?
  D No, not at all.

T 4.10 See p43

T 4.11

1 A Do you think you could give me a lift to the station?
  B I'm terribly sorry, I can't. I have to be at work by 8.30. I'll order you a taxi, though.
2 A Could you possibly help me find my glasses? I can't find them anywhere.
  B Sorry! I'm afraid I have to dash or I'll miss the bus. I'm hopeless at finding things anyway.
3 A Hi! Listen, would you like to come round for a meal tomorrow evening? I'm cooking Chinese.
  B Oh, I'd love to, but I'm afraid I'm already going out.
  A Oh, what a shame! Another time perhaps.
4 A Would you mind lending me your dictionary?
  B I would if I could but I'm afraid I forgot to bring it with me today. Sorry.
5 A Hi, it's Susan here. Could I ask you a big favour? I wonder if you could look after my dog next week? I'm going on holiday.
  B I'm terribly sorry, Susan, but I can't. I'd love to have Molly, you know I adore dogs, but I'm going away myself for a few days.
6 A Do you happen to know where the toilet is?
  B Sorry. I'm afraid I've no idea. Ask the guy serving drinks, he'll know.
7 A Would you like me to help you with this exercise? I think I know the answers.
  B That's really kind of you but I want to try and work it out for myself. Thanks anyway.
8 A Excuse me. Would you mind *not* whistling?
  B I'm sorry. I didn't realize I was.
  A That's OK.

T 4.12

A = Anna, B = Ben, H = Henry
B Kim! Hello! Great to see you. Come on in. Let me take your coat.
Kim Thanks very much. Oh, these are for you.
A What lovely flowers! How kind of you! Thank you so much. Now, I don't think you know Henry? Let me introduce you. Henry, this is Kim.
H Hello, Kim. Nice to meet you. I've heard a lot about you.
Kim Oh, I hope it was all good!
H Where exactly are you from, Kim?
Kim Well, I'm Canadian. I was born in Saskatoon but I've been working in the US for the last couple of years.
H That's interesting. And what are you doing in London?
Kim Work, I'm sorry to say. Actually, I'm on my way to Amsterdam for a conference, and I thought I'd stop over in London to see Anna and Ben. We used to work together in New York.
H And how do you find London, Kim? Is it like home, or is it very different?
Kim Well, it's very different from Saskatoon and New York! I know London quite well, actually, I always love it here.

B Now, Kim. What would you like to drink?
Kim Oh, could I have a beer? No, sorry, I'll have a glass of red wine, if that's OK.
B Right. I'll just get that for you.
Kim Thanks.
A Right, everybody. Dinner's ready. Come and sit down. Kim, can you sit next to Henry?
Kim Yes, of course.
B Has everyone got a drink? Cheers, everybody!
Kim Cheers! It's great to be here.
A Kim, help yourself. Would you like some Parmesan parsnips?
Kim Parmesan parsnips? I don't think I've ever had them. What are they?
A Well, they're parsnips coated in Parmesan cheese and roasted? Would you like to try some?
Kim Well, I'd love to but I'd better not – cheese doesn't always agree with me.
B Another glass of wine, perhaps?
Kim No, I'm alright, thanks very much. But d'you think I could have a glass of water?
B Yes, of course. Sparkling or still?
Kim Just tap water would be fine. That's great Thanks a lot.
A Well, *bon appetit* everyone!

UNIT 5

T 5.1

1 I did my A-levels a few months ago, and I've just got my results. Fortunately, they're good, so I'm going to study psychology at Bristol University. The course lasts three years.
2 It's Saturday tomorrow, so I'm going to see the football with my boy and some mates. Oxford United are playing Bristol Rovers. It'll be a great game. Kick-off is at 3 o'clock, so we'll have a beer or two before the match.
3 Marie's having a baby soon, so we're both very excited. The baby's due in five weeks. If it's a boy, we're going to call him Jamie. And if it's a girl, she'll be Hatty.
4 What am I doing tomorrow, you say? Well, it's Thursday tomorrow, so I'll be doing what I always do on a Thursday. My daughter will come to see me, she'll be bringing the little 'uns, and we'll all have a cup of tea and a good old chat. And I'll bake a cake. A sponge cake with jam in it. They like that.
5 At the moment I'm packing, because tomorrow I'm going to France for a year. I'm going to study literature at the Sorbonne. My plane leaves at 10.30. My mum and dad are taking me to the airport. I have absolutely no idea how I'm going to carry all this lot.
6 Well, I work in the City. In the next few years I'm going to be even more successful. I hope I'll be earning twice what I'm getting now. I've set myself this goal. Before I'm twenty-five I'll have made a million.

T 5.2

1 She's going to study psychology.
  It lasts three years.
2 He's going to a football match.
  The match starts at 3.00.
3 Because they're going to have a baby.
4 Her daughter and grandchildren will be visiting.
  They'll have a cup of tea and a chat.
5 Because she's going to France for a year.
  Her mother and father are taking her.
6 He's going to be successful. He'll be earning a lot of money. He'll have made a million pounds before he's twenty-five.

1 Which university is she going to?
2 Who's he going to the match with? Who's playing?
3 What are they going to call the baby?
4 What sort of cake is she going to bake?
5 What time does her plane leave?
6 How much will he be earning?

T 5.4

1 I'm very excited. I'm going to see all my family this weekend.
   I don't know if I have time to come this evening. I'll see.
2 So you're off to the States for a year! What are you going to do there?
   I'm sure you will pass your exams, but what will you do if you don't?
3 I'll come with you if you like.
   I'm coming with you whether you like it or not.
4 Your school report is terrible. What are you going to do about it?
   What are you doing this evening?
5 I've had enough of her lazy attitude. I'm going to give her a good talking to.
   I'm giving a presentation at 3.00 this afternoon. I'm scared stiff.
6 John! Peter is leaving now. Come and say goodbye.
   The coach leaves at 9.00, so don't be late.
7 I'll see you outside the cinema at 8.00.
   I'll be seeing Peter this afternoon, so I'll tell him your news.
8 You'll have seen enough of me by the end of this holiday.
   I'm going to make a success of my life. You'll see.

T 5.5

This is your captain speaking. Good morning, ladies and gentlemen. Welcome on board this British Airways flight to Rome. In a very short time we'll be taking off. When we've reached our cruising speed of 550 miles per hour, we'll be flying at 35,000 feet. Our flight time today is two and a half hours, so we'll be in Rome in time for lunch. The cabin crew will be serving refreshments during the flight. If you need any assistance, just press the button and a flight attendant will come to help you.
(Near the end of the flight)
In a few moments' time, the crew will be coming round with duty-free goods. We will also be giving out landing cards. When you have filled them in, place them in your passport. They will be collected as you go through passport control. In twenty minutes' time we will be landing at Leonardo da Vinci airport. Please put your seats in the upright position. You are requested to remain seated until the plane has come to a complete standstill. We hope you will fly again soon with British Airways.

T 5.6

1 Do you think you'll ever be rich?
   I hope so.
   I might one day.
   It's possible, but I doubt it.
   I'm sure I will.
   I'm sure I won't.
2 Are you going out tonight?
   Yes, I am.
   I think so, but I'm not sure.
   I might be.
3 Do you think the world's climate will change dramatically in the next fifty years?
   I don't think so.
   I hope not.
   Who knows? Maybe.

T 5.7

1 The wedding took place in an old country church. It was lovely, but it was miles away. It took ages to get there.
2 My son's buying cigarettes, but I'll soon put a stop to that. I won't give him any more pocket money.

3 Please don't take offence, but I don't think your work has been up to your usual standard recently.
4 I told you that boy was no good for you. You should have taken my advice and had nothing to do with him.
5 The older you get, the more you have to learn to take responsibility for your own life.
6 My boss is putting pressure on me to resign, but I won't go.
7 I tried to get the teacher's attention but she took no notice of me at all.
8 Children never say 'Thank you' or 'How are you?' to their parents. They just take them for granted.

T 5.8

1 The shop takes on a lot of extra staff every Christmas.
2 The lecture was too complicated, and the students couldn't take it all in.
3 My business really took off after I picked up six new clients.
4 You called me a liar, but I'm not. Take that back and say sorry!

T 5.9

1 Put some music on. Whatever you want.
2 That article about factory farming has really put me off eating chicken.
3 Could you put away your clothes, please. Your room's a total mess.
4 Put your cigarette out! You can't smoke in here.

T 5.10 **The reunion**

A = Alan   S = Sarah

S Hello. 267890.
A Hello. Is that Sarah?
S Speaking.
A Hi, Sarah. It's Alan, Alan Cunningham.
S Alan! Hi! How are you? How are things?
A OK, yeah, not too bad, thanks. And you? How's the family?
S Oh, we're surviving! Busy, busy, busy, but what's new?
A Tell me about it! Listen, I'm phoning about our reunion ...
S Oh, yes? On the fourteenth, right? Friday night. I can't wait. I'm really looking forward to it.
A Have you any ideas where we can meet? A restaurant somewhere?
S Well, what do you fancy? Indian? A Chinese? There's that really good Chinese we used to go to in Claypath.
A Oh, yes. What's it called?
S The Lotus Garden.
A That's right. Now, I'm driving from the Midlands, so I'll be coming into Durham from the M1. Where can I park?
S There's a car park bang opposite the restaurant.
A That's great. I'll be leaving about 3.00 in the afternoon, so I should be in Durham about 5, 6 o' clock depending on the traffic.
S Where are you staying?
A In The County. What about you?
S Oh, that's good. I'm staying in The Three Tuns, just down the road. We can meet up for a drink.
A Sounds great! How are you getting there?
S By train. It's direct from Leeds, so it's easy. The journey takes less than an hour. I'm getting the 17.05. Why don't I come to The County at about 6.30? I'll see you in the bar.
A All right. That sounds great. Will you phone James, or shall I?
S Erm ... No, don't worry. I'll phone him.
A OK. So I'll see you in the bar of The County on the fourteenth. I presume there's only one.
S Well, it's not that big. I'm sure we won't lose each other!
A True. OK. See you then.
S About 6.30.
A That's it. Bye.
S Bye. Take care.

T 5.11 **The reunion**

J = James   S = Sarah

J Hello. Simpson's Travel Agents.
S Hello, James. This is Sarah Jackson. How are you?
J Sarah! Hello! How lovely to hear from you!
S Sorry to disturb you at work.
J Oh, don't worry. I'm only too pleased to be interrupted. How's everything with you?
S Oh, fine. Have you got a lot on at the moment?
J Well, it's our busy time of year. Still, I mustn't complain.
S That's right. Business is business! Anyway, James, I spoke to Alan yesterday, you know, about our get-together in Durham on the fourteenth, and I'm just ringing to let you know what's happening.
J Great!
S We've decided to meet in the Lotus Garden, the er ... Chinese restaurant ...
J You mean the one in Claypath?
S Yes.
J Where we all used to go?
S Yeah.
J Oh.
S Why? Is that no good?
J Er ... it closed about three years ago.
S Oh, dear. Are you sure?
J Uh huh. Absolutely. But it doesn't matter. There's the other one, the Kwai Lam.
S Now where's that? I've forgotten.
J It's on the corner of Saddler Street.
S Oh, great. OK. Now, how are you coming from Sunderland?
J Well, I'm so close. I'll be catching the bus. The office closes at 6.00, and I'll go straight to the bus station.
S So you'll be there at about ... what? Seven?
J Yeah, something like that.
S Well, look. Why don't we see you in the Kwai Lam? I'm meeting Alan in The County before that, because we both get in earlier than you.
J OK. I'll phone Alan and sort it all out.
S Great. What about if we see you in the Kwai Lam between seven and half past? How does that sound?
J Fine. That'll give me enough time, I'm sure. Shall I phone and book a table?
S Good idea. By the way, where are you staying that night?
J I'm going to phone a friend of mine to see if he can put me up for the night.
S Oh, lovely! Well, we'll see you on the fourteenth, then, around 7.15.
J In the restaurant, that's it. And you know where it is, don't you?
S Yeah, yeah, I've got it. Bye, now, James.
J Bye, Sarah. Thanks for phoning.

T 5.12

1 A Hello. The Regent Hotel. Kathy speaking. How can I help you?
   B Hello. I was wondering if I could book a room ...

2 A Hello.
   B Hello, Pat. It's me, Dave.
   A Dave! Hi! How are things?
   B Not bad. Busy, busy, busy, but life's like that. How's everything with you?
   A Oh, you know, we've all got the flu, and Mike's away on business, so I've got to do the lot. School, shop, kids, cook, clean. It's great! What are you up to?
   B This and that ...
   A How's your mother, by the way?
   B She's a lot better, thanks. Really on the mend.

3 Welcome to National Phones. To help us deal with your call more efficiently, please select one of the following options.
   For customer services, press 1. To query a bill, press 2. To request a brochure, press 3.
   To return to the beginning of this menu, press the hash key. To speak to an operator, please hold.

T 5.13

A Hello. TVS Computers. Samantha speaking. How can I help you?
B Good morning. Could I speak to your customer services department, please?
A Certainly. Who's calling?
B This is Keith Jones.
A (*pause*) I'm afraid the line's busy at the moment. Will you hold?
B Yes, please.
A (*pause*) OK. It's ringing for you now.
B Thank you.
C (*ring, ring*) Hello. Customer services.
B Hello. I was wondering if you could help me ...

T 5.14

A So, Barry. It was good to talk to you. Thanks very much for phoning.
B My pleasure. By the way, how's your golf these days? Still playing?
A No, not much. I just don't seem to find the time these days. Anyway, Barry ...
B What a shame! You used to enjoy it so much.
A It's true. Right, Barry. I must fly. I'm late for a meeting.
B OK. Don't want to keep you. So, you'll give me a ring when you're back, right?
A I certainly will. And you'll send me a copy of the report?
B It'll be in the post tonight.
A That's great, Barry. Have a good weekend!
B Same to you, too! Bye, Andy.
A Bye, Barry.

UNIT 6

T 6.1 Jamie Oliver

At only 28, Jamie Oliver is now an extremely successful and well known chef, with his own acclaimed restaurant in the centre of London. He has made quite a few TV series, written four books, and still does a large number of live shows a year. He doesn't have many free days any more. How did he make it big?
Well, his rise to fame and fortune came early and swiftly. By the age of eight he had already started cooking at his parents' pub. It was an easy way to earn a little pocket money! After a couple of years in catering college, and a little time spent in France, he started working in restaurants. He worked under a few famous chefs in London, before he was spotted by a TV producer at 21, and his life changed.
Even though he had hardly any experience, he had a lot of enthusiasm for cooking, and was very natural in front of the camera. His first TV programme featured him zipping around London on his scooter buying ingredients and cooking for his friends, all to a rock and roll soundtrack. The recipes were bare and simple – they didn't involve complicated cooking techniques and used lots of fresh ingredients and herbs. It attracted a completely new audience that previously didn't have any interest in food programmes. Jamie Oliver became an overnight success.
So what's his recipe for success? 'A little bit of luck, a little bit of passion, and a little bit of knowledge!' he says.

T 6.2

1 'How much money have you got in your pocket?'
   'About twenty euros.'
2 'How many cups of coffee do you drink a day?'
   'It depends. I have milky coffee for breakfast, sometimes another mid-morning, then maybe one or two, black, after lunch and dinner.'
3 'How many times have you been on a plane?'
   'About five or six.'
4 'How much time do you spend watching TV?'
   'A couple of hours a night, just before I go to bed, I suppose.'

5 'How much sugar do you have in your coffee?'
   'Just half a spoonful in white coffee, and none in black.'
6 'How many pairs of jeans do you have?'
   'Three. A black pair, a blue pair, and an old pair I wear when I do dirty jobs like cleaning the car.'
7 'How many books do you read in one year?'
   'I honestly don't know. Ten? Fifteen? I read most when I'm on holiday.'
8 'How much homework do you get a night?'
   'Too much! About two hours, maybe? It depends.'
9 'How many English teachers have you had?'
   'Er ... let me see ... about ten, I guess.'
10 'How many films do you watch a month?'
   'One or two in the cinema, and one or two on television.'

T 6.3

1 There's no need to rush. We've got masses of time.
2 She's got bags of money. I think she inherited it.
3 We've got heaps of food for the party. Don't buy any more.
4 When my daughter comes back from university, she always brings piles of washing.
5 I can't see you today. I've got tons of things to do.
6 There were millions of people at the sales. I couldn't be bothered to fight my way through them.

T 6.4 Six radio adverts

1 **S = Sarah M = Mummy**
Sarah is five, and this is her favourite play shirt. It's pink, with fluffy yellow ducks. Sarah loves her play shirt.
S It's my favourite.
And she wears it to play in the garden.
S Look what I've found, Mummy!
And you wash it at low temperature. And she wears it to play in the garden.
S Mummy! Look what I've made!
And you wash it. And she wears it to play in the garden.
M Sarah! What on earth ... ?
And after a while, the dirt builds up, so the pink isn't quite as pink, and the yellow ducks aren't as fluffy. New System Sudso Automatic can help. Its advanced formula can remove ground-in dirt even at low temperatures. So the pink stays very pink, and the fluffy yellow ducks are happy again. Wash ...
S Mummy! Look what I've made!
... after wash ...
S Look what I've found, Mummy!
... after wash ...
M Sarah! Don't you dare bring that in here!
New System Sudso Automatic. It's all you could want from a powder.

2 **A** 'Ere, Bill! Just ... just watch this. Look! Look at that car trying to park!
B Ooh! You're joking! Ooh-ooh! Now that just has to be a woman driver. It must be.
A It's gotta be. 'Ere, do you want some help, love? Hey, look! Look at her now! Look! Look!
B I don't believe it! She's just whacked that GTI! Are you all right, darling?
A It's a bloke.
B Bloke. Oh. It was a tight space, though, wannit, eh? [Oh, yeah.] Really.
A Yeah, that space, very tight space. Yeah.
B Complicated.
Since men are responsible for 81% of parking offences and 96% of dangerous driving offences, why should women have to pay the same for car insurance? At Swinton, we have access to policies with up to 20% reductions for women. For a competitive quote, contact your local branch, or Freefone Swinton on 0800 600 700.

3 **C = Child D = Daddy**
C Daddy! Daddy! Today I did a painting of you! And I got two stars! And Miss Lewis says I was the best in class!
D You're a very naughty girl!

C Why daddy?
D Don't argue with your father, young lady! Now, go to your room ...! It's no use crying about it. Go on! Go on! Get out!
Wednesday's UEFA Champion's League night. Manchester United – Bayern Munich. 7.30. ITV 1. Do not disturb.

4 **D = Daughter F = Father**
D Well, Dad. I've decided which new car I'm getting.
F It's all right for some. When I was your age ...
D ... you counted yourself lucky to have a bike. And that was second-hand.
F Now, well, that's where you're wrong, Miss Smartypants. I was going to say that when I was twenty-two. I couldn't even have afforded to insure a new car.
D Neither can I.
F Well, don't expect me ...
D ... and I don't have to. 'Cos all new Ford Escorts now come with one year's free insurance, for anyone between 18 and 80. Which rules you out, anyway.
See your Thames Ford dealer now, as offer ends soon. Free insurance, subject to age and status.
F Just like your mother. Always have to have the last word.
D No I don't.

5 Hi, this is Sue. Please leave a message.
Hi Sue. Met you last night. Just wondering if you –er want to meet up sometime. Erm, I'm going away soon, so maybe it could be soon. Er, don't want to sound too keen. Not that I'm not keen, 'cos I am. Well, you know, within reason. Anyway, maybe lunch, or maybe just a drink? Not that you shouldn't do lunch, I mean you're not, you're not fat –er, you're not fat at all actually, you've got a great, –erm ... Not that that's important, it, it's personality that counts. Erm, anyway ...
Have a break. Have a Kit Kat.

6 **P = Priest T = Tony**
P Er–hem! Everyone! Welcome! We're gathered here today, in the presence of others, to marry Tony and Helen. Helen, do you take Tony to be your husband? Just nod. Tony, do you take her?
T I w...
P Lovely rings. Oop! Leave it! Leave it! Kiss! Lovely. Husband and wife. Wife, husband. Right. You're married. Jolly good. I'm outa here.
Come to IKEA after work. But don't rush! We're open till 10 p.m. weeknights.

T 6.5

a	'export	ex'port
b	'import	im'port
c	'decrease	de'crease
d	'increase	in'crease
e	'progress	pro'gress
f	'record	rec'ord
g	'refund	re'fund
h	'produce	pro'duce
i	'permit	per'mit
j	'transport	trans'port
k	'insult	in'sult
l	'protest	pro'test

T6.6

1 Scotland imports a lot of its food from other countries. Its exports include oil, beef, and whisky.
2 I'm very pleased with my English. I'm making a lot of progress.
3 Ministers are worried. There has been an increase in the number of unemployed.
4 But the number of crimes has decreased, so that's good news.
5 How dare you call me a liar and a cheat! What an insult!
6 There was a demonstration yesterday. People were protesting about blood sports.

7 He ran 100m in 9.75 seconds and broke the
   world record.
8 Don't touch the DVD player! I'm recording a film.
9 Britain produces about 50% of its own oil.

T 6.7

a	'refuse	re'fuse
b	'present	pre'sent
c	'minute	min'ute
d	'desert	de'sert
e	'content	con'tent
f	'object	ob'ject
g	'invalid	in'valid
h	'contract	con'tract

T 6.8

1 A refuse collector.
2 An unidentified flying object.
3 A desert in northern Africa.
4 Presents!
5 The contents pages.
6 con'tent   mi'nute
   'contract   re'fuse
   in'valid

T 6.9

1 A Mike! Long time no see! How are things?
   B Good, thanks, Jeff. Business is booming.
      What about yourself?
2 A I'm afraid something's come up, and I can't
      make our meeting on the 6th.
   B Never mind. Let's go for the following week.
      Is Wednesday the 13th good for you?
3 A What are your travel arrangements?
   B I'm getting flight BA 2762, at 18.45.
4 A Could you confirm the details in writing?
   B Sure. I'll email them to you as an attachment.
5 A They want a deposit of $2\frac{1}{2}$ percent, which is
      £7,500, and we ... the two ... thousand ... ge ... t...
   B Sorry, I didn't quite get that last bit. What
      was it again?
6 A I'll give you £5,250 for your car. That's my
      final offer.
   B Great! It's a deal. It's yours.
7 A I don't know their number offhand. Bear
      with me while I look it up.
   B No worries. I'll hold.
8 A OK. Here's their number. Are you ready? It's
      0800 205080.
   B I'll read that back to you. Oh eight double
      oh, two oh five, oh eight oh.
9 A So what's your salary, Dave? 35K? 40K?
   B Hey! Mind your own business! You wouldn't
      tell anyone yours!
10 A Have you applied for that job?
   B There's no point. I'm not qualified for it. I
      wouldn't stand a chance.

T 6.10 See p61

Grammar Reference

UNIT 1

 1.1 The tense system

There are three classes of verbs in English: auxiliary verbs, modal verbs, and full verbs.

1 Auxiliary verbs

The auxiliary verbs are *be*, *do*, and *have*.

be

1 *Be* is used with verb + *-ing* to make continuous verb forms.
*You're **lying**.* (present)
*They **were reading**.* (past)
*I've **been swimming**.* (present perfect)
*We'll **be having** dinner at 8 o'clock.* (future)
*You must **be joking**!* (infinitive)

2 *Be* is used with the past participle to make the passive.
*These books **are printed** in Hong Kong.* (present)
*Where **were** you **born**?* (past)
*The car's **been serviced**.* (present perfect)
*The city **had been destroyed**.* (past perfect)
*This work should **be done** soon.* (infinitive)

do

1 *Do/does/did* are used in the Present Simple and the Past Simple.
***Do** you smoke?* (question)
*She **doesn't** understand.* (negative)
*When **did** they arrive?* (question)

2 *Do/does/did* are used to express emphasis when there is no other auxiliary.
*I'm not interested in sport, but I **do** like tennis.*
*'If only she had a car!' 'She **does** have a car!'*
*'Why didn't you tell me?' 'I **did** tell you!'*

have

Have is used with the past participle to make perfect verb forms.
***Have** you ever **tried** sushi?* (present)
*My car **had broken** down before.* (past)
*I'll **have finished** soon.* (future)
*I'd like **to have met** Napoleon.* (infinitive)
***Having had** lunch, we tidied up.* (participle)

> **have and have got**
>
> 1 *Have* and *have got* are both used to express present possession.
>
> **Do** you **have**
> **Have** you **got** | *any brothers or sisters?*
>
> *Yes,* | *I **do**. I **have***
> *I **have**. I've **got*** | *two brothers.*
>
> 2 *Have to* can be replaced with *have got to* for present obligation.
>
> **Do** you **have to**
> **Have** you **got to** | *go now?*
>
> *Yes,* | *I **do**. I **have to***
> *I **have**. I've **got to*** | *catch the bus.*

3 Only forms of *have* (not *have got*) are used in all other tenses.
*I **had** my first car when I was nineteen.*
*I've **had** this car for two years.*
*I'll **have** a strawberry ice-cream, please.*
*I'd **had** three cars by the time I was twenty.*
*I'd like **to have** a dog.*
*He loves **having** a sports car.*

4 *Have* (not *have got*) is used in many expressions.

have breakfast	*have a bath*
have a party	*have a good time*
have fun	*have a word with someone*

5 *Have got* is generally more informal. It is used more in spoken English than in written English. However, they are often interchangeable.
Have with the *do/does* forms is more common in American English.

Other uses of auxiliary verbs

1 In question tags.
*It's cold today, **isn't** it?*
*You don't understand, **do** you?*
*You haven't been to China, **have** you?*

2 In short answers. *Yes* or *No* alone can sound abrupt.
*'Are you hungry?' 'No, **I'm not**.'*
*'Do you like jazz?' 'Yes, **I do**.'*
*'Did you have a nice meal?' 'Yes, **we did**.'*
*'Has she seen the mess?' 'No, **she hasn't**.'*

3 In reply questions. These are not real questions. They are used to show that the listener is paying attention and is interested. They are practised on p33 of the Student's Book.
*'The party was awful.' '**Was it**? What a pity.'*
*'I love hamburgers.' '**Do you**? I hate them.'*
*'I've bought you a present.' '**Have you**? How kind!'*

2 Modal auxiliary verbs

These are the modal auxiliary verbs.

can	could	may	might	will	would
shall	should	must	ought to		need

They are auxiliary verbs because they 'help' other verbs. They are different from *be*, *do*, and *have* because they have their own meanings.
*He **must** be at least 70.* (= probability)
*You **must** try harder.* (= obligation)
***Can** you help me?* (= request)
*She **can't** have got my letter.* (= probability)
I'll help you. (= willingness)
*(Ring) That'**ll** be the postman.* (= probability)
Modal auxiliary verbs are dealt with in Units 5, 7, 9, 10, and 11.

3 Full verbs

Full verbs are all the other verbs in the language.

run	walk	eat	love	go	talk	write

The verbs *be*, *do*, and *have* can also be used as full verbs with their own meanings.
*Have you **been** to school today?*
*I want **to be** an engineer.*
*I **do** a lot of business in Russia.*
*The holiday **did** us a lot of good.*
*They're **having** a row.*
*Have you **had** enough to eat?*

1.2 English tense usage

English tenses have two elements of meaning: time and aspect.

Time

1 The time referred to is usually obvious.
*English people **drink** tea.* (all time)
*Shh! I'm **watching** this programme!* (now)
*I'll **see** you later.* (future)
*I **went** out with Jenny last night.* (past)

2 Sometimes a present tense form can refer to the future.
*I'm **going** out tonight.* (Present Continuous for near future)
*The train **leaves** at 10.00 tomorrow.* (Present Simple for a timetable)
*If you **see** Peter, say hello from me.* (Present Simple in a subordinate clause)

3 Sometimes a past tense form can refer to the present.
*I wish I **could** help you, but I can't.*
This use of unreal tense usage is dealt with in Unit 11.

The simple aspect

1 The simple aspect describes an action that is seen to be complete. The action is viewed as a whole unit.
*The sun **rises** in the east.* (= all time)
*When I've **read** the book, I'll lend it to you.* (= complete)
*She **has** red hair.* (= permanent)
*He always **wore** a suit.* (= a habit)
*It **rained** every day of our holiday.* (= the whole two weeks)
*This shop **will close** at 7.00 this evening.* (= a fact)

2 Remember the verbs that rarely take the continuous. This is because they express states that are seen to be permanent and not subject to frequent change.

Verbs of the mind	know understand believe think mean
Verbs of emotions	love hate like prefer care
Verbs of possession	have own belong
Certain other verbs	cost need contain depend

3 The simple aspect expresses a completed action. For this reason we must use the simple, not the continuous, if the sentence contains a number that refers to 'things done'.
*She's **written three** letters this morning.*
*I **drink ten** cups of tea a day.*
*He **read five** books while he was on holiday.*
Simple tenses are dealt with further in Units 2, 3, and 5.

The continuous aspect

1 The continuous aspect focuses on the duration of an activity. We are aware of the passing of time between the beginning and the end of the activity. The activity is not permanent.
*I'm **staying** with friends until I find a flat.* (= temporary)
*What **are** you **doing** on your hands and knees?* (= in progress)
*I've **been learning** English for years.* (And I still am.)
*Don't phone at 8.00. We'll **be eating**.* (= in progress)

2 Because the activity is seen in progress, it can be interrupted.
*We **were walking** across a field when we were attacked by a bull.*
*'**Am I disturbing** you?' 'No. I'm just **doing** the ironing.'*

3 The activity may not be complete.
*I **was writing** a report on the flight home.* (I didn't finish it.)
*He **was drowning**, but we saved him.* (He didn't die.)
*Who's **been drinking** my beer?* (There's some left.)

4 The action of some verbs, by definition, lasts a long time, for example, *live, work, play*. The continuous gives these actions limited duration and makes them temporary.
*Hans **is living** in London while he's **learning** English.*
*I'm **working** as a waiter until I go to university.*
*Henman **has been playing** well recently. Maybe he'll win Wimbledon.*

5 The action of some other verbs lasts a short time, for example, *lose, break, cut, hit, crash*. They are often found in the simple.
*I **lost** all my money.*　　*I've **crashed** your car. Sorry.*
*She's **cut** her finger.*　　*He **hit** me.*
In the continuous, the action of these verbs seems longer or habitual.
*I've **been cutting** the grass.* (= for hours)
*He **was hitting** me.* (= again and again)

Note
We cannot say a sentence such as *I've been crashing your car* because it suggests an activity that was done deliberately and often.
Continuous tenses are dealt with further in Units 2, 3, and 5.

The perfect aspect

The perfect aspect expresses two ideas.

1 The action is completed before another time.
***Have** you ever **been** to America?* (= some time before now)
*When I arrived, Peter **had left**.* (= some time before I arrived)
*I'll **have finished** the report by 10.00.* (= some time before then)

2 The exact time of the verb action is not important. The perfect aspect refers to indefinite time.
***Have** you **seen** my wallet anywhere? I've **lost** it.* (= before now)
*We'll **have arrived** by this evening.* (= before this evening)
The exception to this is the Past Perfect, which *can* refer to definite time.
*I recognized him immediately. I **had met** him **in 1992** at university.*
Perfect tenses are dealt with further in Units 2, 3, and 5.

Active and passive

1 Passive sentences move the focus of attention from the subject of an active sentence to the object.
***Shakespeare** wrote Hamlet in 1599.*
***Hamlet**, one of the great tragedies, was written in 1599.*

2 In most cases, *by* and the agent are omitted in passive sentences. This is because the agent is not important, isn't known, or is understood.
My car was stolen yesterday.
This house was built in the seventeenth century.
She was arrested for shoplifting.

3 Sometimes we prefer to begin a sentence with what is known, and end a sentence with what is 'new'. In the passive, the 'new' can be the agent of the active sentence.
*'What a lovely painting!' 'Yes. It was painted **by Canaletto**.'*

4 In informal language, we often use *you* or *they* to refer to people in general or to no person in particular. In this way we can avoid using the passive.
***You** can buy anything in Harrods.*
***They**'re building a new airport soon.*

5 There are many past participles that are used more like adjectives.
*I'm very **impressed** by your work.*
*You must be **disappointed** with your exam results.*
*I'm **exhausted**! I've been on my feet all day.*
Passive sentences are dealt with further in Unit 3.

UNIT 2

Introduction to the Present Perfect

1 Many languages have a past tense to refer to past time, and a present tense to refer to present time. English has these, too, but it also has the Present Perfect, which relates past actions to the present.

2 The use of the Past Simple roots an action in the past, with no explicit connection to the present. When we come across a verb in the Past Simple, we want to know *When?*

3 The use of the Present Perfect always has a link with the present. When we come across a verb in the Present Perfect, we want to know how this affects the situation now.

4 Compare these sentences.
*I **lived** in Rome.* (But not any more.)
*I**'ve lived** in Rome, Paris, and New York.* (I know all these cities now.)
*I**'ve been living** in New York for ten years.* (And I'm living there now.)
*She**'s been married** three times.* (She's still alive.)
*She was **married** three times.* (She's dead.)
***Did** you **see** the Renoir exhibition?* (It's finished now.)
***Have** you **seen** the Renoir exhibition?* (It's still on.)
***Did** you **see** that programme on TV?* (I'm thinking of the one that was on last night.)
***Did** you **enjoy** the film?* (Said as we're leaving the cinema.)
***Have** you **enjoyed** the holiday?* (Said near the end of the holiday.)
*Where **have** I **put** my glasses?* (I want them now.)
*Where **did** I **put** my glasses?* (I had them a minute ago.)
*It **rained** yesterday.* (= past time)
*It**'s been snowing**.* (There's snow still on the ground.)

Present Perfect Simple and Continuous

See the introduction to the perfect aspect and the continuous aspect in Unit 1. These tenses have three main uses.

1 Unfinished past

The verb action began in the past and continues to the present. It possibly goes on into the future, as well.
*We**'ve lived** in this house for twenty years.*
*Sorry I'm late. **Have** you **been waiting** long?*
*I**'ve been** a teacher for five years.*
*I**'ve been working** at the same school all that time.*

Notes

- There is sometimes little or no difference between the simple and the continuous.
  *I**'ve played***
  *I**'ve been playing*** *tennis since I was a kid.*

- The continuous can sometimes suggest a more temporary situation. The simple can sound more permanent.
  *I**'ve been living** with a host family for six weeks.*
  *The castle **has stood** on the hill overlooking the sea for centuries.*

- Certain verbs, by definition, suggest duration, for example, *wait, rain, snow, learn, sit, lie, play, stay.* They are often found in the continuous.
  *It**'s been raining** all day.*
  *She**'s been sitting** reading for hours.*

- Remember that state verbs rarely take the continuous.
  *I**'ve known** Joan for years.* *I've been knowing
  *How long **have** you **had** that car?* *have you been having
  *I**'ve never understood** why she likes him.* *I've never been understanding

2 Present result

The verb action happened in the past, usually the recent past, and the results of the action are felt now.
*You**'ve changed**. What **have** you **done** to yourself?*
*I**'ve lost** some weight.*
*I**'ve been doing** some exercise.*
*I'm covered in mud because I**'ve been gardening**.*
In this use, the simple emphasizes the completed action. The continuous emphasizes the repeated activities over a period of time.

Notes

- Certain verbs, by definition, suggest a short action, for example, *start, find, lose, begin, stop, break, die, decide, cut.* They are more often found in the simple.
  *We**'ve decided** to get married.*
  *I**'ve broken** a tooth.*
  *I**'ve cut** my finger.*
  In the continuous, these verbs suggest a repeated activity.
  *I**'ve been stopping** smoking for years.*
  *You**'ve been losing** everything lately. What's the matter with you?*
  *I**'ve been cutting** wood.*

- The use of the simple suggests a completed action.
  *I**'ve painted** the bathroom.*
  The use of the continuous suggests a possibly incomplete action.
  *I'm tired because I**'ve been working**.* (Finished? Not finished?)
  *Someone**'s been drinking** my beer.* (There's some left.)

- The continuous can be found unqualified by any further information.
  *I'm wet because I**'ve been swimming**.*
  *We're tired because we**'ve been working**.*
  *'Why are you red?' 'I**'ve been running**.'*
  The simple sounds quite wrong in this use.
  *I've swum. *We've worked. *I've run.

- Sometimes there is little difference between the Past Simple and the Present Perfect.
  Where | *did you put* | *my keys?*
           | *have you put* |

- American English is different from British English. In American English, these sentences are correct.
  Did you hear the news? The President resigned!
  Did you do your homework yet?
  Your father just called you.
  I had breakfast already.

3 Indefinite past

The verb action happened at an unspecified time in the past. The actual time isn't important. We are focusing on the experience at some time in our life.
*Have you ever **taken** any illegal drugs?*
*She**'s** never **been** abroad.*
*Have you ever **been flying** in a plane when it's hit an air pocket?*

Note

- Notice these two sentences.
  *She**'s been** to Spain.* (At some time in her life.)
  *She**'s gone** to Spain.* (And she's there now.)
  The first is an example of indefinite past.
  The second is an example of present result.

UNIT 3

 Narrative tenses

Past Simple and Present Perfect

See the introduction to the perfect aspect and the simple aspect on p80. The Past Simple differs from all three uses of the Present Perfect.

1 The Past Simple refers to **finished past**.
   *Shakespeare **wrote** plays.* (He's dead.)
   *I've **written** short stories.* (I'm alive.)

2 There is **no present result**.
   *I **hurt** my back.* (But it's better now.)
   *I've **hurt** my back.* (And it hurts now.)

3 It refers to **definite past**.

I saw him	last night.
	two weeks ago.
	on Monday.
	at 8.00.

Compare this with the indefinite adverbials found with the Present Perfect.

| *I've seen him* | recently. |
| | before. |

I haven't seen him	since January.
	yet.
	for months.

| *I've* | never | seen him. |
| | just | |

Note

Even when there is no past time adverbial, we can 'build' a past time in our head.
***Did you have** a good journey?* (The journey's over. You're here now.)
*Thank you for supper. It **was** lovely.* (The meal is finished.)
*Where **did you buy** that shirt?* (when you were out shopping the other day.)

Past Simple

The Past Simple is used:

1 to express a finished action in the past.
   *Columbus **discovered** America in 1492.*

2 to express actions which follow each other in a story.
   *I **heard** voices coming from downstairs, so I **put on** my dressing-gown and **went** to investigate.*

3 to express a past state or habit.
   *When I **was** a child, we **lived** in a small house by the sea. Every day I **walked** for miles on the beach with my dog.*

This use is often expressed with *used to*.
*We **used to live** ...*
*I **used to walk** ...*
See Unit 9 for more information on *used to*.
See Unit 11 for information on the Past Simple used for hypothesis.

Past Continuous

See the introduction to the continuous aspect on p80.
The Past Continuous is used:

1 to express an activity in progress before and probably after a time in the past.
   *I phoned at 4.00, but there was no reply. What **were** you **doing**?*

2 to describe a past situation or activity.
   *The cottage **was looking** so cosy. A fire **was burning** in the grate, music **was playing**, and from the kitchen **were coming** the most delicious smells.*

3 to express an interrupted past activity.
   *I **was having** a bath when the phone rang.*

4 to express an incomplete activity in the past.
   *I **was reading** a book during the flight.* (But I didn't finish it.)
   *I **watched** a film during the flight.* (the whole film)

5 to express an activity that was in progress at every moment during a period of time.
   *I **was working** all day yesterday.*
   *They **were fighting** for the whole of the holiday.*

Notes

- The Past Simple expresses past actions as simple, complete facts. The Past Continuous gives past activities time and duration.
  'What did you do last night?'
  *'I **stayed** at home and **watched** the football.'*
  'I phoned you last night, but there was no reply.'
  *'Oh, I **was watching** the football and I didn't hear the phone. Sorry.'*

- Notice how the questions in the Past Continuous and Past Simple refer to different times.
  When we arrived, Jan was ironing. She stopped ironing and made some coffee.
  *What **was** she **doing** when we arrived? She was ironing.*
  *What **did** she **do** when we arrived? She made some coffee.*

Past Perfect

See the introduction to the perfect aspect and the continuous aspect on p80.
The Past Perfect is used to look back to a time in the past and refer to an action that happened before then.
*She was crying because her dog **had died**.*
*I arrived to pick up Dave, but he **had already left**.*
*Keith was fed up. He'**d been looking** for a job for months, but he'**d found** nothing.*

Notes

- The continuous refers to longer actions or repeated activities. The simple refers to shorter, complete facts.
  *He'**d lost** his job and his wife **had left** him. Since then he'**d been sleeping** rough, and he **hadn't been eating** properly.*

- The Past Perfect can refer to definite as well as indefinite time.
  *I knew his face immediately. I'**d first met** him **in October 1993**.* (= definite)
  *I recognized her face. I'**d seen** her somewhere **before**.* (= indefinite)

Past Perfect and Past Simple

1 Verbs in the Past Simple tell a story in chronological order.
*John **worked** hard all day to prepare for the party. Everyone **had** a good time. Even the food **was** all right. Unfortunately, Andy **upset** Peter, so Peter **left** early. Pat **came** looking for Peter, but he **wasn't** there.*
*It **was** a great party. John **sat** and **looked** at all the mess. He **felt** tired. It **was** time for bed.*

2 By using the Past Perfect, the speaker or writer can tell a story in a different order.
*John sat and looked at all the mess. It **had been** a great party, and everyone **had had** a good time. Even the food **had been** all right. Unfortunately, Andy upset Peter, so Peter left early. Pat came looking for Peter, but he'**d already gone**.*
*John felt tired. He'**d been working** all day to prepare for the party. It was time for bed.*

Note
For reasons of style, it is not necessary to have every verb in the Past Perfect.
*... Andy upset Peter … Peter **left** ...*
Once the time of 'past in the past' has been established, the Past Simple can be used as long as there is no ambiguity.

Time clauses

1 We can use time conjunctions to talk about two actions that happen one after the other. Usually the Past Perfect is not necessary in these cases, although it can be used.
*After I'd **had/had** a bath, I **went** to bed.*
*As soon as the guests **left/had left**, I **started** tidying up.*
*I **sat** outside until the sun **had gone/went** down.*

2 The Past Perfect can help to make the first action seem separate, independent of the second, or completed before the second action started.
*When I **had read** the paper, I threw it away.*
*We stayed up until all the beer **had gone**.*

3 Two verbs in the Past Simple can suggest that the first action led into the other, or that one caused the other to happen.
*When I **heard** the news, I **burst** out crying.*
*As soon as the alarm **went off**, I **got up**.*

4 The Past Perfect is more common with *when* because it is ambiguous. The other conjunctions are more specific, so the Past Perfect is not so essential.
*As soon as all the guests **left**, I tidied the house.*
*Before I **met** you, I didn't know the meaning of happiness.*
*When I **opened** the door, the cat jumped out.*
*When I'**d opened** the mail, I made another cup of tea.*
See Unit 11 for information on the Past Perfect used for hypothesis.

UNIT 4

4.1 Questions

Question forms
Notice these question forms.

- Subject questions with no auxiliary verb
  ***Who broke** the window?*
  ***What happens** at the end of the book?*

- Questions with prepositions at the end
  ***Who** is your letter **from**?*
  ***What** are you talking **about**?*

- Question words + noun/adjective/adverb
  ***What sort** of music do you like?*
  ***How big** is their new house?*
  ***How fast** does your car go?*

- Other ways of asking *Why?*
  ***What** did you do that **for**?*
  ***How come** you got here before us?*
  How come …? expresses surprise. Notice that there is no inversion in this question form.

what and which

1 *What* and *which* are used with nouns to make questions.
   ***What size** shoes do you take?*
   ***Which of these curries** is the hottest?*

2 Sometimes there is no difference between questions with *what* and *which*.
   ***What/which is the biggest city** in your country?*
   ***What/which channel** is the match on?*

3 We use *which* when the speaker has a limited number of choices in mind.
   *There's a blue one and a red one. **Which** do you want?*
   We use *what* when the speaker is not thinking of a limited number of choices.
   ***What car** do you drive?*

Asking for descriptions

1 *What is X like?* means Give me some information about X because I don't know anything about it.
   ***What**'s your capital city **like**?*
   ***What** are your parents **like**?*

2 *How is X?* asks about a person's health and happiness.
   ***How**'s your mother these days?*
   Sometimes both questions are possible. *What ... like?* asks for objective information. *How ... ?* asks for a more personal reaction.
   *'**What** was the party **like**?' 'Noisy. Lots of people. It went on till 3.'*
   *'**How** was the party?' 'Brilliant. I danced all night. Met loads of great people.'*
   ***How** was your journey?*
   ***How**'s your new job going?*
   ***How**'s your meal?*

Indirect questions
There is no inversion and no *do/does/did* in indirect questions.
*I wonder what she's doing. *I wonder ~~what is she doing~~.*
*I don't know where he lives. *I don't know ~~where does he live~~.*
Tell me when the train leaves.
Do you remember how she made the salad?
I didn't understand what she was saying.
I've no idea why he went to India.
I'm not sure where they live.
He doesn't know whether he's coming or going.

4.2 Negatives

Forming negatives

1 We make negatives by adding *not* after the auxiliary verb. If there is no auxiliary verb, we add *do/does/did*.
   *I **haven't** seen her for ages.*
   *It **wasn't** raining.*
   *You **shouldn't** have gone to so much trouble.*
   *We **don't** like big dogs.*
   *They **didn't** want to go out.*

2 The verb *have* has two forms in the present.
   *I **don't** have | any money.*
   *I **haven't** got*
   But ... *I **didn't** have any money.*

3 Infinitives and *-ing* forms can be negative.
   *We decided **not to do** anything.*
   *I like **not working**. It suits me.*

4 *Not* can go with other parts of a sentence.
   *Ask him, **not me**.*
   *Buy me anything, but **not perfume**.*

5 When we introduce negative ideas with verbs such as *think, believe, suppose,* and *imagine*, we make the first verb negative, not the second.
   *I **don't think** you're right.* *I think you aren't ...*
   *I **don't suppose** you want a game of tennis?*

6 In short answers, the following forms are possible.

   Are you coming?' | *'I think so.'*
   | *'I believe so.'*
   | *'I hope so.'*
   | *'I don't think so.'*
   | *'I hope not.'*

   I think not is possible. *I don't hope so* is not possible.

Negative questions

1 Negative questions can express various ideas.
   Haven't you finished school yet? (surprise)
   Don't you think we should wait for them? (suggestion)
   Wouldn't it be better to go tomorrow? (persuasion)
   Can't you see I'm busy? Go away! (criticism)
   Isn't it a lovely day! (exclamation)

2 In the main use of negative questions, the speaker would normally expect a positive situation, but now expresses a negative situation. The speaker therefore is surprised.
   Don't you like ice-cream? Everyone likes ice-cream!
   Haven't you done your homework yet? What have you been doing?

3 Negative questions can also be used to mean *Confirm what I think is true*. In this use it refers to a positive situation.
   Haven't I met you somewhere before? (I'm sure I have.)
   Didn't we speak about this yesterday? (I'm sure we did.)

4 The difference between the two uses can be seen clearly if we change them into sentences with question tags.
   You haven't done your homework yet, have you? (negative sentence, positive tag)
   We've met before, haven't we? (positive sentence, negative tag)

UNIT 5

Introduction to future forms

There is no one future tense in English. Instead, there are several verb forms that can refer to future time. Sometimes, several forms are possible to express a similar meaning, but not always.

will for prediction

1 The most common use of *will* is as an auxiliary verb to show future time. It expresses a future fact or prediction – *at some time in the future this event will happen*. This use is uncoloured by ideas such as intention, decision, arrangement, willingness, etc.
   I'll be thirty in a few days' time.
   It will be cold and wet tomorrow, I'm afraid.
   Who do you think will win the match?
   You'll feel better if you take this medicine.
   I'll see you later.
   This is the nearest English has to a neutral, pure future tense.

2 *Will* for a prediction can be based more on an opinion than a fact or evidence. It is often found with expressions such as *I think ..., I hope ..., I'm sure ...* .
   I think Labour will win the next election.
   I hope you'll come and visit me.
   I'm sure you'll pass your exams.

3 *Will* is common in the main clause when there is a subordinate clause with *if, when, before,* etc. Note that we don't use *will* in the subordinate clause.
   You'll break the glass if you aren't careful.
   When you're ready, we'll start the meeting.
   I won't go until you arrive.
   As soon as Peter comes, we'll have lunch.

going to for prediction

Going to can express a prediction based on a present fact. There is evidence now that something is sure to happen. We can see the future from the present.
Careful! That glass is going to fall over. Too late!
Look at that blue sky! It's going to be a lovely day.

Notes

• Sometimes there is little or no difference between *will* and *going to*.
   We'll | *run out of money if we aren't careful.*
   We're going to |

• We use *going to* when we have physical evidence to support our prediction.
   She's going to have a baby. (Look at her bump.)
   Liverpool are going to win. (It's 4–0, and there are only five minutes left.)
   That glass is going to fall. (It's rolling to the edge of the table.)

• We can use *will* when there is no such outside evidence. Our prediction is based on our own personal opinion. It can be more theoretical and abstract.
   I'm sure you'll have a good time at the party. (This is my opinion.)
   I reckon Liverpool will win. (Said the day before the match.)
   The glass will break if it falls. (This is what happens to glasses that fall.)

• Compare the sentences.
   I bet John will be late home. The traffic is always bad at this time. (= my opinion)
   John's going to be late home. He left a message on the answerphone. (= a fact)
   Don't lend Keith your car. He'll crash it. (= a theoretical prediction)
   Look out! We're going to crash! (= a prediction based on evidence)

Decisions and intentions – *will* and *going to*

1 *Will* is used to express a decision or intention made at the moment of speaking.

I'll phone you back in a minute.
Give me a ring some time. We'll go out together.
'The phone's ringing.' 'I'll get it.'

2 *Going to* is used to express a future plan, decision, or intention made before the moment of speaking.

When she grows up, she's going to be a ballet dancer.
We're going to get married in the spring.

Other uses of *will* and *shall*

1 *Will* as a prediction is an auxiliary verb that simply shows future time. It has no real meaning.

Tomorrow will be cold and windy.

2 *Will* is also a modal auxiliary verb, and so it can express a variety of meanings. The meaning often depends on the meaning of the main verb.

I'll help you carry those bags. (= offer)
Will you marry me? (= willingness)
Will you open the window? (= request)
My car won't start. (= refusal)
I'll love you for ever. (= promise   'The phone's ringing.'*
'It'll be for me.' (= prediction about the present)

3 *Shall* is found mainly in questions. It is used with *I* and *we*.

Where shall I put your tea? (I'm asking for instructions.)
What shall we do tonight? (I'm asking for a decision.)
Shall I cook supper tonight? (I'm offering to help.)
Shall we eat out tonight? (I'm making a suggestion.)

Present Continuous for arrangements

1 The Present Continuous is used to express personal arrangements and fixed plans, especially when the time and place have been decided. A present tense is used because there is some reality in the present. The event is planned or decided, and we can see it coming. The event is usually in the near future.

I'm having lunch with Brian tomorrow.
What time are you meeting him?
Where are you having lunch?
What are you doing tonight?

2 The Present Continuous for future is often used with verbs of movement and activity.

Are you coming to the dance tonight?
I'm meeting the director tomorrow.
I'm just taking the dog for a walk.
We're playing tennis this afternoon.

3 The Present Continuous is used to refer to arrangements between people. It is not used to refer to events that people can't control.

It's going to rain this afternoon. *It's raining this afternoon.
The sun rises at 5.30 tomorrow. *The sun is rising ...

Notes

• Sometimes there is little or no difference between the Present Continuous and *going to* to refer to the future.

We're seeing
We're going to see | *Hamlet at the theatre tonight.*

• When there is a difference, the Present Continuous emphasizes an arrangement with some reality in the present; *going to* expresses a person's intentions.

I'm seeing my girlfriend tonight.
I'm going to ask her to marry me. *I'm asking ...
What are you doing this weekend?
What are you going to do about the broken toilet? (= What have you decided to do?)

Present Simple for timetables

1 The Present Simple refers to a future event that is seen as unalterable because it is based on a timetable or calendar.

My flight leaves at 10.00.
Term starts on 4 April.
What time does the film start?
It's my birthday tomorrow.

2 It is used in subordinate clauses introduced by conjunctions such as *if, when, before, as soon as, unless,* etc.

We'll have a picnic if the weather stays fine.
When I get home, I'll cook the dinner.
I'll leave as soon as it stops raining.

Future Continuous

1 The Future Continuous expresses an activity that will be in progress before and after a time in the future.

Don't phone at 8.00. We'll be having supper.
This time tomorrow I'll be flying to New York.

2 The Future Continuous is used to refer to a future event that will happen in the natural course of events. This use is uncoloured by ideas such as intention, decision, arrangement, or willingness. As time goes by, this event will occur.

Don't worry about our guests. They'll be arriving any minute now.
We'll be going right back to the football after the break. (said on television)

Future Perfect

The Future Perfect refers to an action that will be completed before a definite time in the future. It is not a very common verb form.

I'll have done all my work by this evening.

UNIT 6

 Expressing quantity

Quantifiers

1 The following can be used before a noun.

| some/any much/many each/every more/most |
| a little/little a few/few both fewer/less several |
| all/no enough |

With count nouns only	With uncount nouns only	With both count and uncount nouns
(not) many cigarettes a few cars very few trees fewer books several answers	(not) much luck a little cheese very little experience less time	some money some eggs (not) any water (not) any friends more/most wine more/most people all/no work all/no children enough food enough apples

With singular count nouns only	With plural count nouns only
each boy every time	both parents

2 Most of the quantifiers can be used without a noun. *No, all, every,* and *each* cannot.

Have you got any money?   **Not much/a little/enough**.
Are there any eggs?   **A few/not many**.
Have some wine.   *I don't want* **any**.
How many people came?   *Very* **few**.
Have some more tea.   *I've got* **some**.
Did Ann or Sam go?   **Both**.

3 Most of the quantifiers can be used with *of + the/my/those*, etc. + noun. *No* and *every* cannot.

They took **all of my money**.
Take **a few of these tablets**.
Some of the people *at the party started dancing.*
Were **any of my friends** *at the party?*
Very **few of my friends** *smoke.*
Not **much of the food** *was left.*
I've missed **too many of my French lessons**.
I couldn't answer **several of the questions**.
I'll have **a little of the strawberry cake**, *please.*
Both of my children *are clever.*
I feel tired **most of the time**.
I've had **enough of your jokes**.

4 For *no* and *every*, we use *none* and *every one* or *all*.

None of the audience *was listening.*
All of the hotels *were booked.*

In formal, written English, *none* is followed by a singular form of the verb.

None of the guests has *arrived yet.*

But in informal English, a plural verb is possible.

None of my friends smoke.
None of the lights are *working.*

Note

When we use *none* with a plural noun or pronoun, the verb can be singular or plural. Grammatically, it should be singular, but people often use the plural when they speak.

None of my friends **is** *coming.*
None of my friends **are** *coming.*

some, any, somebody, anything

1 The basic rule is that *some* and its compounds are used in affirmative sentences, and *any* and its compounds in negatives and questions.

I need **some** *help.*
I need **somebody** *to help me.*
Give me **something** *for my headache.*
I don't need **any** *shopping.*
We can't go **anywhere** *without being recognized.*
Is there **any** *sugar left?*
Did **anyone** *phone me last night?*

2 *Some* and its compounds are used in requests or invitations, or when we expect the answer 'yes'.

Have you got **some** *money you could lend me?*
Would you like **something** *to eat?*
Did **someone** *phone me last night?*
Can we go **somewhere** *quiet to talk?*

3 *Any* and its compounds are used in affirmative sentences that have a negative meaning.

He **never** *has* **any** *money.*
You made **hardly any** *mistakes.*
I made the cake myself **without any** *help.*

4 *Any* and its compounds are used to express *It doesn't matter which/who/where.*

Take **any book** *you like. I don't mind.*
Anyone *will tell you 2 and 2 makes 4.*
Sit **anywhere** *you like.*
I eat **anything**. *I'm not fussy.*

nobody, no one, nowhere, nothing

1 These are more emphatic forms.

I saw **nobody** *all weekend.*
I've eaten **nothing** *all day.*

2 They can be used at the beginning of sentences.

No one *was saved.*
Nobody *understands me.*
Nowhere *is safe any more.*

much, many, a lot of, lots of, a great deal of, a large number of, plenty of

1 *Much* and *many* are usually used in questions and negatives.

How much *does it cost?*
How many *people came to the party?*
Is there **much** *unemployment in your country?*
I don't have **much** *money.*
Will there be **many** *people there?*
You don't see **many** *snakes in England.*

2 We find *much* and *many* in affirmative sentences after *so, as,* and *too.*

He has **so much** *money that he doesn't know what to do with it.*
She hasn't got **as many** *friends as I have.*
You make **too many** *mistakes. Be careful.*

3 In affirmative sentences, the following forms are found.

Spoken/informal

There'll be **plenty of food/people**. (uncount and count)
We've got **lots of time/friends**. (uncount and count)
I lost **a lot of my furniture/things**. (uncount and count)

Written/more formal

A great deal of money *was lost during the strike.* (uncount)
A large number of strikes *are caused by bad management.* (count)
Many world leaders *are quite young.* (count)
Much time *is wasted in trivial pursuits.* (uncount)

4 These forms are found without nouns.

'Have you got enough socks?' **'Lots.'**
'How many people were there?' **'A lot.'**
Don't worry about food. We've got **plenty**.

little/few/less/fewer

1 *A little* and *a few* express a small amount or number in a positive
   way. Although there is only a little, it is probably enough.
   *Can you lend me **a little sugar**?*
   ***A few friends** are coming round tonight.*

2 *Little* and *few* express a small amount in a negative way. There is not
   enough.
   ***Very few people** passed the exam.*
   *There's **very little milk** left.*

3 *Fewer* is the comparative of *few*, *less* is the comparative of *little*.
   ***Fewer people** go to church these days.* (= count noun)
   *I spend **less and less time** doing what I want to.* (= uncount noun)
   It is becoming more common to find *less* with a count noun. Many
   people think that this is incorrect and sounds terrible.
   *Less people go to church.
   *You should smoke less cigarettes.

all

1 We do not usually use *all* to mean *everybody/everyone/everything*.
   ***Everybody** had a good time.*
   ***Everything** was ruined in the fire.*
   *I said hello to **everyone**.*
   But if *all* is followed by a relative clause, it can mean *everything*.
   ***All** (that) I own is yours.*
   *I spend **all** I earn.*
   This structure can have a negative meaning, expressing ideas such as
   nothing more or *only this*.
   ***All I want** is a place to sleep.*
   ***All I had** was a couple of beers.*
   ***All that happened** was that he pushed her a bit, and she fell over.*

2 Before a noun with a determiner (for example *the*, *my*, *this*) both *all*
   and *all of* are possible.
   *You eat **all (of) the time**.*
   ***All (of) my friends** are coming tonight.*
   Before a noun with no determiner, we use *all*.
   ***All people** are born equal.*

3 With personal pronouns, we use *all of*.
   ***All of you** passed. Well done!*
   *I don't need these books. You can have **all of them**.*

Extra material

 UNIT 1 *p15*

EVERYDAY ENGLISH
Social expressions and the music of English
T 1.12

A Excuse me, is this yours?

B Let me see. Yes, it is. Thank you. I must have dropped it.

A Are you going far?

B Yeah, all the way to London. What about you?

A I'm getting off at Bristol.

B Oh, d'you live there?

A Actually, no. I work in Bristol but I live in Bath.

B Lucky you! I think Bath's a beautiful city!

A Yeah, you and thousands of others!

B What d'you mean?

A Well, you know, the tourists. There are just so many, all year round.

B Ah yes, that's a drag. You don't like tourists then?

A Well, I shouldn't really complain.

B How come? You can complain if you want.

A Not really – you see I'm a travel agent, so I make a living from tourists.

 UNIT 2 *p18*

PRACTICE
Exchanging information

Student A

Ask and answer questions to complete the information about Tony and Maureen Wheeler.

> How many people does it employ?

> Five hundred. Where does it have offices?

> In the USA, France, England, and Australia.

lonely planet

Lonely Planet is one of the outstanding publishing successes of the past three decades. It employs more than . . . people (*How many?*), and has offices in the USA, France, England, with its headquarters in Melbourne, Australia.

Tony and Maureen Wheeler have been writing *Lonely Planet* guide books for . . . (*How long?*). They have written more than 650 guides. They sell . . . copies a year (*How many?*) in 118 countries. The books have been translated into 17 languages.

Tony lived . . . (*Where?*) when he was young because his father's job took him all over the world. He studied . . . at Warwick University (*What?*), then business studies at the London Business School.

Maureen was born in . . . (*Where?*). She went to London at the age of 20 because she wanted to see the world. Three days later she met Tony . . . (*Where?*). In 1972 they travelled overland across Europe, through Asia, and on to Australia. The trip took six months. They wrote their first book, called . . . (*What?*), on their kitchen table in Melbourne. They have lived in Melbourne on and off for over thirty years.

Together they have been to . . . countries (*How many?*). Tony says that the most amazing place he has ever visited is a remote hilltop city called Tsaparang, in Tibet.

They are currently travelling in . . . (*Where?*), researching a new edition of their guide to the country.

He is thinking of selling . . . (*What?*). He said, 'I've had a wonderful time, it's been terrific, but it has now got too much like a business.'

Venture to a higher plain

PRACTICE
Exchanging information

Student B
Ask and answer questions to complete the information about Tony and Maureen Wheeler.

> How many people does it employ?

> Five hundred. Where does it have offices?

> In the USA, France, England, and Australia.

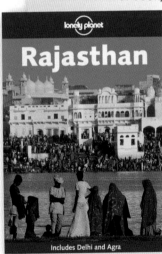

Lonely Planet is one of the outstanding publishing successes of the past three decades. It employs more than 500 people, and has offices in . . . *(Where?)*, with its headquarters in Melbourne, Australia.

Tony and Maureen Wheeler have been writing *Lonely Planet* guide books for over thirty years. They have written . . . guides *(How many?)*. They sell around 5.5 millions copies a year in 118 countries. The books have been translated into . . . languages *(How many?)*.

Tony lived in many different countries when he was young because . . . *(Why?)*. He studied engineering at Warwick University, then business studies at . . . *(Where?)*.

Maureen was born in Belfast. She went to London at the age of 20 because . . . *(Why?)*. Three days later she met Tony on a bench in Regent's Park. In 1972 they travelled overland across Europe, through Asia, and on to Australia. The trip took . . . *(How long?)*. They wrote their first book, called *Across Asia on the cheap*, on their kitchen table in Melbourne. They have lived in Melbourne on and off for over . . . *(How long?)*.

Together they have been to more than 100 countries. Tony says that the most amazing place he has ever visited is . . . *(What?)*.

They are currently travelling in India, . . . *(What . . . doing . . . ?)*

He is thinking of selling his shares in the company. He said, '. . .' *(What?)*.

PRACTICE
Exchanging information

Information for Tony Wheeler

BACKGROUND
- Father worked for British Airways
- Lived in Pakistan, Bahamas, USA
- Lived overseas for most of my school days

EDUCATION
- Educated mainly in Britain and the USA, most of my secondary education was in the States
- Came back to England to do my A-levels when I was 16
- Went to Warwick University to study engineering

WORK
- Started a career in engineering, did this for a couple of years in Coventry
- Went to do an MBA in business studies in London

LONELY PLANET GUIDES
- First one came out in 1973
- Idea came because a lot of people were asking us questions about our trip across Asia
- Worst moment was when we first started the business. We didn't have enough money
- Best moment was doing something that no one had done before. Our guides were the first of their kind
- The secret of our success is that people can rely on us, so they keep coming back to us.
- If you want to get into travel writing, you have to have travelled a lot. You have to be able to write well. You have to believe in what you're doing. Wanting to do it is far more important than wanting to make money

FAMILY
- Two children, a girl and a boy

HOLIDAYS
- Like walking and diving

FUTURE
- Would like to go back to Nepal.
- Am looking forward to spending a long time in Australia. In my opinion, there's no better place in the world to be alone

UNIT 2 *p22*

SPEAKING AND LISTENING

Dreams come true

These are the top 15 things that people most wanted to do before they die.

1 swim with dolphins
2 go scuba diving on the Great Barrier Reef
3 go whale-watching
4 dive with sharks
5 go skydiving
6 fly in a hot air balloon
7 fly in a fighter jet
8 go on safari
9 see the Northern Lights
10 visit Machu Picchu
11 climb Sydney Harbour Bridge
12 escape to a paradise island
13 drive a Formula-1 car
14 go white-water rafting
15 walk the Great Wall of China

UNIT 3 *p28*

PRACTICE

News and responses

Student A
Read the newspaper story. Then tell the story to your partner. Show him/her the photo.

GIRL BARRED FROM TOP STORE

As fashion-conscious GILLY WOODWARD left Harrods last Friday, she felt proud of the £120 designer jeans that she had just bought. But when Gilly, 31, returned to the store the next day to do some more shopping, she was barred from entry because she was wearing the same jeans.

Gilly, now back home in Liverpool, had been staying with friends in London for a few days. She explained what had happened.

'I was walking through the swing doors, when suddenly I was stopped by a large, uniformed security guard. He pointed at my knees, and said that my jeans were torn and I couldn't enter. I tried to tell him that I had bought them in Harrods the day before, and that the torn bits were fashionable. But he didn't listen. He told me to get out. By this time, a crowd of people had gathered. I left immediately because I had never felt so embarrassed in my life.'

A spokesperson from Harrods said that the dress code had been introduced in 1989, and it states: no beachwear, no backpacks, no torn denims.

 UNIT 4 *p35*

PRACTICE

Quiztime!

Group A

Music
1 Louis Armstrong played <u>jazz</u> music. (*What sort?*)
2 A violin has <u>four</u> strings. (*How many?*)

Sports
3 <u>A bronze medal</u> is given to the person who comes third in the Olympic Games. (*What?*)
4 Golf was first played in <u>Scotland</u>. (*In which?*)

Science
5 <u>The sun</u> is the nearest star to the earth? (*Which?*)
6 <u>Albert Einstein</u> developed the theory of relativity. (*Who?*)

Geography
7 The capital of <u>New Zealand</u> is Wellington. (*Which country?*)
8 The 'Richter Scale' measures <u>earthquakes</u>. (*What?*)

History
9 President John F. Kennedy was assassinated in <u>1963</u>. (*Which year?*)
10 Nelson Mandela was in prison for <u>twenty-eight</u> years. (*How long ... for?*)

PRACTICE
News and responses

Student B
Read the newspaper story. Then tell the story to your partner. Show him/her the photo.

Man fined for keeping tiger in apartment

A MAN WHO kept a 400-pound tiger in his apartment in Harlem, New York, has been fined $2,500, and forbidden from keeping animals for ten years.

Brian Jackson, 31, had bought the Bengal tiger, named Ming, when it was just a three-month-old cub. It had been living in his fourth-floor apartment for three years, eating raw meat provided by Jackson, who worked as a butcher. Neighbours had often complained of strange smells and loud noises.

Jackson's unusual pet came to light because he had had to go to hospital with cuts and bites to his arm. The tiger had attacked him in an apparent attempt to capture and kill a cat that he also kept in the apartment.

Police officers scaled down the outside of the building and fired tranquilizer darts through an open fourth-floor window. They removed the tiger, and also an alligator, to a New York animal shelter.

A neighbour said, 'We liked having Ming here. He was cool. My worry is that he won't like the country. He's a city cat, and likes jazz and hip-hop.'

 UNIT 4 *p35*

PRACTICE
Quiztime!

Group B

Music
1 Eminem sings <u>rap</u> music. *(What kind?)*
2 <u>Michael Jackson's</u> brothers formed the pop group 'The Jackson Five.' *(Whose?)*

Sports
3 <u>The Marathon</u> is the longest running race in the Olympic Games. *(What ... called?)*
4 Baseball was first played in <u>the United States</u> in the <u>19th century</u>. *(Where and when?)*

Science
5 A butterfly has <u>six</u> legs. *(How many?)*
6 Charles Darwin developed <u>the theory of evolution</u>. *(Which theory?)*

Geography
7 <u>Alaska</u> is the biggest state in the US. *(Which state?)*
8 <u>The Atlantic and Pacific Oceans</u> are linked by the Panama Canal. *(Which oceans?)*

History
9 President John F. Kennedy was assassinated in <u>Dallas, Texas</u>. *(Which town and state?)*
10 The last Concorde flew to New York in <u>2003</u>. *(In which year?)*

EVERYDAY ENGLISH
Roleplay

A = Anna   **B** = Ben   **H** = Henry   **K** = Kim

B Kim! Hello! Great to see you. Come on in. Let me take your coat.

K Thanks very much. Oh, these are for you.

A What lovely flowers! How kind of you! Thank you so much. Now, I don't think you know Henry? Let me introduce you. Henry, this is Kim.

H Hello, Kim. Nice to meet you. I've heard a lot about you.

K …

H Where exactly are you from, Kim?

K …

H That's interesting. And what are you doing in London?

K …

H And how do you find London, Kim? Is it like home, or is it very different?

K …

B Now, Kim. What would you like to drink?

K …

B Right. I'll just get that for you.

K …

A Right, everybody. Dinner's ready. Come and sit down. Kim, can you sit next to Henry?

K …

B Has everyone got a drink? Cheers, everybody!

K …

A Kim, help yourself. Would you like some Parmesan parsnips?

K …

A Well, they're parsnips coated in Parmesan cheese and roasted. Would you like to try some?

K …

B Another glass of wine, perhaps?

K …

B Yes, of course. Sparkling or still?

K …

A Well, *bon appétit* everyone!

READING AND SPEAKING

Nobody listens to us

These are the ten social issues that the group of 18–24 year-olds cared about, in order of importance.

1 Improving the NHS
2 Ensuring equal rights and protections for everyone, regardless of gender, sexual orientation, colour, or religion
3 Reducing crime levels
4 Raising standards in schools
5 Improving public transport
6 Ending the arms trade
7 Addressing the causes of global warming
8 Redistributing wealth from the richest to the poorest
9 Increasing the amount of aid we give to developing countries
10 Ending globalization

Phonetic symbols

Consonants

1	/p/	as in	**pen**	/pen/
2	/b/	as in	**big**	/bɪg/
3	/t/	as in	**tea**	/tiː/
4	/d/	as in	**do**	/duː/
5	/k/	as in	**cat**	/kæt/
6	/g/	as in	**go**	/gəʊ/
7	/f/	as in	**four**	/fɔː/
8	/v/	as in	**very**	/'veri/
9	/s/	as in	**son**	/sʌn/
10	/z/	as in	**zoo**	/zuː/
11	/l/	as in	**live**	/lɪv/
12	/m/	as in	**my**	/maɪ/
13	/n/	as in	**near**	/nɪə/
14	/h/	as in	**happy**	/'hæpi/
15	/r/	as in	**red**	/red/
16	/j/	as in	**yes**	/jes/
17	/w/	as in	**want**	/wɒnt/
18	/θ/	as in	**thanks**	/θæŋks/
19	/ð/	as in	**the**	/ðə/
20	/ʃ/	as in	**she**	/ʃiː/
21	/ʒ/	as in	**television**	/'telɪvɪʒn/
22	/tʃ/	as in	**child**	/tʃaɪld/
23	/dʒ/	as in	**German**	/'dʒɜːmən/
24	/ŋ/	as in	**English**	/'ɪŋglɪʃ/

Vowels

25	/iː/	as in	**see**	/siː/
26	/ɪ/	as in	**his**	/hɪz/
27	/i/	as in	**twenty**	/'twenti/
28	/e/	as in	**ten**	/ten/
29	/æ/	as in	**stamp**	/stæmp/
30	/ɑː/	as in	**father**	/'fɑːðə/
31	/ɒ/	as in	**hot**	/hɒt/
32	/ɔː/	as in	**morning**	/'mɔːnɪŋ/
33	/ʊ/	as in	**football**	/'fʊtbɔːl/
34	/uː/	as in	**you**	/juː/
35	/ʌ/	as in	**sun**	/sʌn/
36	/ɜː/	as in	**learn**	/lɜːn/
37	/ə/	as in	**letter**	/'letə/

Diphthongs (two vowels together)

38	/eɪ/	as in	**name**	/neɪm/
39	/əʊ/	as in	**no**	/nəʊ/
40	/aɪ/	as in	**my**	/maɪ/
41	/aʊ/	as in	**how**	/haʊ/
42	/ɔɪ/	as in	**boy**	/bɔɪ/
43	/ɪə/	as in	**hear**	/hɪə/
44	/eə/	as in	**where**	/weə/
45	/ʊə/	as in	**tour**	/tʊə/

OXFORD
UNIVERSITY PRESS

Great Clarendon Street, Oxford OX2 6DP

Oxford University Press is a department of the University of Oxford.
It furthers the University's objective of excellence in research, scholarship,
and education by publishing worldwide in

Oxford New York

Auckland Cape Town Dar es Salaam Hong Kong Karachi
Kuala Lumpur Madrid Melbourne Mexico City Nairobi
New Delhi Shanghai Taipei Toronto

With offices in

Argentina Austria Brazil Chile Czech Republic France Greece
Guatemala Hungary Italy Japan Poland Portugal Singapore
South Korea Switzerland Thailand Turkey Ukraine Vietnam

OXFORD and OXFORD ENGLISH are registered trade marks of
Oxford University Press in the UK and in certain other countries

ISBN-13: 978 0 19 439299 0   Complete edition
ISBN-13: 978 0 19 439304 1   Student's Book A
ISBN-13: 978 0 19 439305 8   Student's Book B

ISBN-10: 0 19 439299 6   Complete edition
ISBN-10: 0 19 439304 6   Student's Book A
ISBN-10: 0 19 439305 4   Student's Book B

Printed in Spain by Gráficas Estella

ACKNOWLEDGEMENTS

The authors would like to thank Charles Lowe for his valuable contribution
to the development of this project, and in particular for his ideas on the
Music of English.

The authors and publisher are grateful to those who have given permission to reproduce
the following extracts and adaptations of copyright material: p10 'Expat e-mail:
Chile' by Ian Walker-Smith, BBC News, 11 February 2003. Reproduced by
permission of BBC. pp30-31 from The Blind Assassin by Margaret Atwood.
Copyright © O. W. Toad Ltd., 2000. Reproduced with permission of Curtis
Brown Group Ltd.; Doubleday, a division of Random House, Inc.; and
McClelland & Stewart Ltd., The Canadian Publishers. p48 'Nobody Listens to
Us' by Damian Whitworth & Carol Midgley, The Times, 30 October 2003
© D Whitworth and C Midgley. Reproduced by permission of NI Syndication.
p67 'Meet the Kippers' by Ray Connolly, Daily Mail, 18 November 2003.
Reproduced by permission of Atlantic Syndication. pp74-75 'Fall asleep and
you'll freeze to death' by Sarah Oliver, Mail on Sunday, 23 November 2003.
Reproduced by permission of Atlantic Syndication. pp90-91 The American
West 1840-1895 by Mike Mellor © Cambridge University Press, 1998.
Reproduced by permission of Cambridge University Press. p92 Jim And The
Lion from Cautionary Verses by Hilaire Belloc. Reprinted by permission of PFD
on behalf of The Estate of Hilaire Belloc © The Estate of Hilaire Belloc, 1930.
p106-107 'A Life in the Day of Mary Hobson' by Caroline Scott, The Sunday
Times Magazine, 30 November 2003. Reproduced by permission of NI
Syndication. p108 That's Life Words & Music by Dean Kay & Kelly Gordon
© Copyright 1964 Bibo Music Publishers, USA. Universal Music Publishing
Limited. All Rights Reserved. International Copyright Secured. p122 'A
Darwin Award, Larry was a Truck Driver' from www.tech-sol.net as shown on
14 June 2004. Reproduced by permission of Mike Guenther, Techsol.

Sources: pp102-103 Based on copyright material 'How's your timing' by Celia
Brayfield.

Location art directors: Sally Smith and Mags Robertson

Art editing by: Pictureresearch.co.uk

Illustrations by: Derek Brazell p 72; Gill Button p 93; Stuart Briers p 31;
CartoonBank p 61 (Thursday's out/© The New Yorker Collection 1993 Robert
Mankoff from cartoonbank.com. All rights reserved); Cartoon Stock
pp 13 (homework/Vahan Shirvanian), (home made/Chris Patterson),
23 (Carroll Zahn), 42 (Mike Baldwin), 51 (Roy Nixon), 68 (snake/Grizelda),
(TV/Tony Hall), 81 (Timmy/Aaron Bacall), 101 (John Morris); Stefan Chabluk
pp 10, 12, 16, 17, 74, 86; Mark Duffin p 122; Paul Gilligan/Getty Images
pp 34 & 35; Illustrations from "Jim" in Cautionary Tales for Children by Hilaire
Belloc, illustrations copyright © 2002 by The Estate of Edward Gorey,
reproduced by permisson of Harcourt Inc & Donadio & Olson Inc pp 92 & 93;
Andy Hammond pp 8, 84; John Holder p 89; Tim Maars pp 100, 158.

Commissioned Photography by: Dennis Kitchen Studio p 6; Gareth Boden pp 43,
44 (Mickey), 45 (Janine), 52 (Students), 67 (Martin), 77 (all except Tattoo), 94,
95 (football); MM Studios pp 14 (pillow, wallet, teabags, straighteners, coffee,
newspapers), 26 (mobile), 29, 32 (banknotes) 77 (Tattoo), 113 (mobile),
117 (Fair Trade produce);

We are grateful to the following for providing locations and props: Roger Noel & the
children's football club, Forest Side Sports Ground p 95; Oselli Ltd, Witney
p 94; Oxford United Football Club p 44; Annie Price, Traffic Warden p 94;
Travelcare Travel Agents, Thame p 94.

We would also like to thank the following for permission to reproduce the following
photographs: The Advertising Archives p 47 (India), (Côte D'Azur), (Chamonix);
AKG-Images p 16 (manuscript illumination, Paris, studio of the Boucicaut
master, c.1412. Paris, Bibliotheque Nationale); Alamy pp 19 (Uluru/D. &
J.Heaton/SC Photos), 22 (northern lights/D.Tipling/ImageState), 22 (rafting/
G.Pearl/StockShot), (jet/R.Cooke), (Great Wall/View Stock China), (shark/
J.Rotman), 26 (falls/J.Agarwal/SCPhotos), 41 (funeral/Popperfoto), 46 (Wagner),
54 (J.Angerson), 60 (acestock), 64 (Miranda/J.Morgan), (Central Park/F.Skold),
111 (Van Hilversum), 113 (J.Cleare/Worldwide Picture Library), 116
(J.Greenberg), 117 (burger/Widmann/f1online), 155 (shark/J.Rotman),
(jet/R.Cooke); Alamy royalty free pp 14 (radio/Ablestock/Hemera Technologies),
81 (teacher/SuperStock), 95 (student/D.Hammond/Design Pics Inc.),
121 (Iwish); Associated Press pp 26 (man/T.McMullen), 156; BBC Photo Library
p 28; Capital Pictures p 83 all; Central News p 27 (schoolboy/E. Wilcox); John
Cleare Mountain Camera pp 26 (mountain), 113 (mountain); John Connor
Press Associates p 32 (S.Dennett); Corbis pp 11 (R.Ressmeyer), 16 (camels/
K.Su), 19 (Thailand/C.Lisle), (Kilimanjaro/T.Davis), (Venice/S.Pitamitz),
20 (A.Cooper), 22 (dolphin/B. Krist), 24, 37 (biscuits/R.Faris), (boy looking up
at mother/N.Schaefer), (boy with report/J-L. Pelaez Inc.), 38 (Bettmann),
39 (Diana/Tim Graham/ Sygma), (Newspapers/Tim Graham), 41 (JFK
Jr/Reuters), 45 (Katrina/J.Woodcock/Reflections Photolibrary), 50 (H.King),
52 (cathedral/A.Woolfitt), 53 (Barry - red tie/S.Prezant), (Andy – blue
shirt/T.McGuire), 57 (D.H.Wells), 59 (B. Ward), 63 (women in bar/LWA-
S.Welstead), 65 (Indian wedding/J.Wishnetsky), 69 (Bettmann), 73
(Russia/S.Sherbell/SABA), 74 (M.Finn-Kelcey), 75 (Chukotka/N.Fobes),
80 (H. Armstrong Roberts), 86 (snow/Corbis Sygma), 90 (Seth Eastman, The
Buffalo Hunter/ G.Clements), 112 (S.Maze), 114 (Bettmann), 123 (detail from
The Creation of Adam by Michelangelo Buonarroti/World Films Enterprises),
155 (dolphin/B.Krist); Empics p 74 (ChelseaFC/EPA); pp 7 (Sophie & Catherine/
J.Slater), 7 (tourists/D.Hiser), 9 (Tokyo/Adastra), 14 (motorbike/E.Fitkau),
14 (cats/W.Eastep), 19 (Greece/G.Hellier), 22 (racing car/P.Rondeau), 25 (eating/
S.Stickler), 33 (S.Krouglikoff), 36 (D.Durfee), 37 (girl in coat/T.Corney),
44 (Elsie/A.Upitis), 45 (Gavin/Chabruken), 53 (woman/S. Cohen), 56 (D.Sacks),
58 (S.Chernin/Stringer), 61 (businessmen/D.Lees), 63 (forgive & forget/H. Grey),
63 (boys/T.Vine), 65 (wedding line-up/B.Thomas), 66 (Vicki & father/K.Webster),
67 (Bill & Judy/T.Schmidt), 76 (crowd/M.Powell), 79 (Hulton Archive), 81 (30's
teacher/W.Vanderson/Stringer/Hulton Archive), 85 (Chabruken),
88 (G.& M-D.de Lossy), 89 (painter/A.Roberts), 103 (R.Daly), 105 (couple/D.Pizzi),
105 (bench/Creaps), 105 (guitar/N.Daly), 110 (J-L.Batt), 119 (theatres/A.Lyon),
120 (S.Justice); Pal Hansen p 107; JoongAng Ilbo, Seoul with special thanks to
Chun Su-jin p 12; Courtesy of Maureen, Tony & Tashi Wheeler and Lonely
Planet Guides pp 18, 19, 24, 153, 154; NASA p 40 (astronauts); National
Pictures p 27 (Rachel de Kelsey); NI Syndication p 49 (The Times/R.Cannon);
Peter Newark p 16 (Marco Polo), 91; Punchstock pp 9 (Kirsty/Photodisc),
15 (Photodisc Green), 17 (Digital Vision), 44 (Tony/Thinkstock), 62 (Comstock),
65 (drive-in wedding/Brand X Pictures), 65 (Pratima/Comstock), 67 (Sandra/
Thinkstock), 96 (Photodisc Green), 98 (Photodisc Red), 115 (Dynamic
Graphics Group / Creatas), 119 (Soho), 119 (Piccadilly/Goodshoot), 153 (on
train); Jacket cover of The Blind Assassin by Margaret Atwood. Used by
permission of Doubleday, a division of Random House Inc; Redferns
p 108 (BBC); Rex Features pp 55 (T.Buckingham), 70 (Silver Image), 71 (S.Cook),
76 (Oscar/D.Lewis); Robin Scagell/Galaxy Picture Library p 40 (moon rock/
Johnson Space Centre); Science Photo Library pp 10 (Observatory/D.Nunuk),
40 (Moon/NASA), 105 (grandfather and child/Maximilian Stock Ltd); Liz Soars
p 105 (sea tractor); South Tyrol Museum of Archaeology, Bolzano www.iceman.it
pp 86 (Iceman model), 87, 157; Still Pictures p 73 (pyramids/H.Schwarzbach)